Battling Eight Giants

Battling Eight Giants

Giants

Basic Income Now

Guy Standing

I.B.TAURIS
LONDON • NEW YORK • OXFORD • NEW DELHI • SYDNEY

I.B. TAURIS

Bloomsbury Publishing Plc

50 Bedford Square, London, WC1B 3DP, UK

1385 Broadway, New York, NY 10018, USA

BLOOMSBURY, I.B. TAURIS and the I.B. Tauris logo are trademarks of
Bloomsbury Publishing Plc

First published in Great Britain 2020

Reprinted 2020

Copyright © Guy Standing, 2020

For legal purposes the Acknowledgements on p. vi constitute an extension of
this copyright page.

Cover design by Adriana Brioso

A catalogue record for this book is available from the British Library.

A catalogue record for this book is available from the Library of Congress.

ISBN: PB: 978-0-7556-0063-2
ePDF: 978-0-7556-0065-6
eBook: 978-0-7556-0064-9

Typeset by Deanta Global Publishing Services, Chennai, India

Printed and bound in Great Britain

To find out more about our authors and books visit www.bloomsbury.com and
sign up for our newsletters.

Contents

Acknowledgements

This book, based on a report written for the Shadow Chancellor of the Exchequer John McDonnell, draws on the support and advice of many people, and has involved presentations and discussions around the country, as well as extensive discussion online and via email. While the author is entirely responsible for the contents, he would like to thank the following in particular: Patrick Allen, Jamie Cooke, Sebastian Corbyn, Geoff Crocker, Marcia Gibson, Louise Haagh, Max Harris, Mark Harrison, Barb Jacobson, Elliott Johnson, Matthew Johnson, Becca Kirkpatrick, Stewart Lansley, Neal Lawson, Rory Macqueen, James Meadway, Annie Miller, Kweku Amonoo-Quyst, Anthony Painter, Mary Partington, Howard Reed, Mary Robertson, Malcolm Torry, Paul Vaughan, Karen Webber, Alan Wheatley, Frances Williams and Charlie Young. Special thanks are due to Anthony Painter and Malcolm Torry who read and commented on the draft report.

He would also like to thank the organizers for meetings in Belfast, Biddulph (Stoke), Birmingham, Brighton, Cambridge, Coventry, Dunfermline, Glasgow, Hull, Keele, Lewes, London, Sheffield and York, and audiences at the Hay Festival.

Special thanks are due to Patrick Allen and the Progressive Economy Forum, which provided financial assistance for the report.

1

Slaying giants with basic income

What is basic income? At its core, it would be a modest regular payment to each individual to help them feel more secure and able to purchase necessities for living.

There is nothing in the concept itself to say how much it should be and nothing to say it should be paid instead of any other policy or that it should be financed by a steep rise in income tax, although obviously the funds would have to come from somewhere. Of course, at some stage one has to say how much should be paid, why it is desirable and even necessary, what are the answers to commonly stated objections and how it could be afforded. Answering these points is the main purpose of this book.

There are many reasons for wanting a basic income system, some uniquely modern, some that stem from way back in our history, first enunciated in *The Charter of the Forest* of 1217. One of the two foundational documents of the British Constitution, the other being the Magna Carta sealed on the same day, the charter asserted that everybody had a *right of subsistence* from 'the commons'. This is a human or citizenship right, not something dependent on specific behaviour or some indicator of worthiness, or merit.

This book argues that the primary reasons for a basic income are ethical and moral. Although basic income would be a more effective means of reducing poverty and inequality than the current system, introducing basic income is first and foremost a matter of social justice. The wealth and income of all of us are due far more to the efforts and achievements of the many generations who came before us, than they are to what we do ourselves. If we accept the practice of private inheritance, as all governments have done, which in its simplest terms gives a lot of 'something for nothing' to a minority, then we should also honour the principle of social inheritance.

If we accept the existence of 'the commons', which I would define as the common resources and amenities, natural or social in origin, bequeathed to us as a society, then we should accept that over the centuries – and egregiously during the austerity era – there has been organized plunder of the commons by privileged private interests at the cost of all of us as commoners.[1] Seen in this way, those who have gained from this plunder should compensate commoners in general for the loss.

As we are all commoners, the compensation should be paid to all, equally and without behavioural conditions. Thomas Paine, writing in the late eighteenth century, best captured this principle – that we all own the wealth of the land, the ultimate commons. So, we might call this the Painian Principle.

A second ethical justification is that, however modest the amount, a basic income would enhance personal and community freedom. It would strengthen the ability of people to say 'no' to exploitative or oppressive employers and to continuation of abusive personal relationships. And it would strengthen what is often called 'republican freedom', the ability to make decisions without having to ask permission from persons in positions of power. It would not do this wholly but would be a move in that direction. One way of putting it is that the emancipatory value of a basic income, by expanding freedom, would be greater than its money value – the opposite of most social policies, which reduce freedom.[2]

The third ethical justification is that it would provide every recipient, and their families and communities, with basic security. Security is a natural public good – you having it does not deprive me of it, and we all gain if others have it too. Whereas too much security can induce 'carelessness' and indolence, lack of basic security reduces the ability to make rational decisions and threatens health and well-being.

A basic income would also strengthen social solidarity, including human relations: it would be an expression that we are all part of a national community, sharing the benefits of the national public wealth created over our collective history. It is essential to revive the ethos of social solidarity that has been eroded in recent decades by excessive individualism and competition.

Although a basic income would be paid individually, it is not individualistic. Being quasi-universal and equal, unlike means-tested social assistance or tax credits, basic income would discourage 'us and them' divisions and confirm that all of us are of equal worth. Though paid to all individuals as equals, its benefits would also be social, offering to improve intra-family relationships, community cohesion and national solidarity.

This book emanated from a report requested as a contribution to policy development by the Shadow Chancellor of the Exchequer. It begins by defining a basic income, then considers the unique combination of pressures that make it almost imperative for any progressive or ecologically principled government to wish to implement it. The book recognizes that a system with a basic income at its base would represent a principled reversal of the trend towards means-testing, behaviour-testing and sanctions that has evolved into Universal Credit (UC). Accordingly, it includes a critique of that trend, along with a critique of similar policy directions regarding disability benefits. Those who are critical of basic income should tell us what alternative they would propose or say they accept UC for what it is.

To be clear from the outset, this book advocates a strategy with the following features:

(1) It would reduce poverty and inequality substantially and sustainably.

(2) It would make nobody in the bottom half of the income distribution system worse off.

(3) It would enhance economic security across the country.

(4) It would not involve any dramatic increase in income taxation.

(5) It would not involve any dismantling of public social services and would be compatible with a strategy to achieve desperately needed public service regeneration after the savage depredations of austerity.

(6) It would reduce the number of people dependent on, and subject to, means-testing and behaviour-testing.

(7) It would contribute positively to the urgent fight against ecological decay.

Defining basic income

Let us start by defining a basic income, bearing in mind that the primary objective is to improve lives while helping to build a twenty-first-century income distribution system that would leave nobody who is currently economically insecure worse off. The defining aspects of a basic income are as follows:

Basic. It would be an amount that would make a significant difference to the income of those currently earning or receiving low incomes. It would provide some basic security, but by no means total security. The amount could start at a low level and rise as resources are mobilized and as experience with the impact grows.

Cash. It would be delivered in money form or in some acceptable substitute, provided people are free to spend the income as they wish. So, it would not be paternalistic, dictating choice, as vouchers or food stamps do, for example.

Regular and predictable. The money would be paid at regular intervals, probably monthly, automatically as a right. This contrasts with uncertain means-tested and behaviour-tested benefits that must be applied for, can vary in value month to month and may be reduced or withdrawn altogether. The perceived value to the recipient would thus be greater than the same amount if paid via means-tests and behaviour-tests.

Individual. It would be paid to every individual regardless of gender, race, marital or household status, income or wealth, employment status or disability. It would be paid equally to men and women, with – in principle – a lower amount for each child under the age of 16 that would go to the mother or primary carer. It is important that it would not be paid according to household or family status, since that is a behavioural matter.

Nothing in the concept of basic income precludes additional supplements to cover special needs. The intention is to provide everybody with equal basic security. So, anybody with a medically accepted disability involving extra costs of living and/or a lower probability of being able to earn income should receive a 'disability benefit' on top of the basic income. However, unlike current policies, the entitlement should be based solely on medical criteria and likely costs, and not on means-tests and arbitrary capacity-to-work tests.

Means-test: an examination into someones financial state to determine their ability to eligibility for public assistance.

Unconditional. The basic income would be paid without the imposition of behavioural conditions such as job-seeking. Research shows that making benefits conditional on certain behaviours is counterproductive and results in the penalization and punishment of vulnerable people and minorities. The basic income would be unconditional in terms of past activity, present activity and future use of the money.

Quasi-universal. The basic income would be payable to every legal resident, though with a delay in entitlement for legal migrants. To avoid potential confusion and misrepresentation, this book will not employ the widely used terms 'universal' and 'citizens' basic income': the basic income would not be paid to everybody coming to Britain nor to every UK citizen, since the several million living and working abroad would be excluded. Citizens' entitlement should be restricted to those who are *usually resident* in the country.

The term 'citizens' basic income' implies that non-citizens living and working in Britain would be excluded, which would be unfair. A simple pragmatic rule could be entitlement after legal residence for at least two years. Beyond that, if the UK remained in the European Union, entitlement would have to accord with EU law.

Claims that a basic income would induce 'welfare tourism' by migrants are unfounded. A means-tested system, like the one operated in Britain in recent years, does worse in this respect, since it effectively puts those most in 'need' at the front of the queue. As recent migrants are among the most needy, a perception is easily (albeit falsely) conveyed that they are gaining at locals' cost. This does not mean that other migrants, refugees and asylum-seekers should be ignored altogether; their needs should be covered by other schemes.

Non-withdrawable. The basic income would be payable to all those entitled and would not be withdrawn as income or personal circumstance changed, as is the case with means-tested benefits.[3] Subject only to change by parliamentary legislation, it would be a *permanent* right.

Although there is no need for the basic income to replace any existing benefit, its introduction would automatically result in a reduction in public spending, since some recipients of means-tested benefits would be lifted above the threshold of entitlement. Even they would gain because, as noted earlier, a *certain* benefit is worth more than an *uncertain* one of the same amount.

There are two forms of basic income considered in this book. One refers to a regular cash payment that substitutes for some other state benefits and subsidies. This is the form commonly considered in analytical and empirical work in Britain, notably by the Citizen's Basic Income Trust. Usually a 'revenue neutral' constraint is imposed, meaning that the basic income is paid for by rolling back some means-tested benefits and subsidies and by raising income tax rates.

The second form is more radical and involves paying an additional benefit, which may be called a common dividend. This rests on the premise that every usually resident citizen and legally accepted migrant is entitled to a share of the collective accumulated wealth of the country and to compensation for loss of the commons – common resources beginning with the land, water and air, extending to our inherited social amenities and bodies of ideas – that should belong to all of us equally. The dividend could be paid from a Commons Fund, built up from levies on commercial exploitation of the commons, which would head off criticism that people with jobs would be taxed more to pay benefits for 'non-workers'. Basic income could even be depicted as integral to a system of 'dividend capitalism', or as 'eco-socialism', depending on one's political preference.

Why is basic income needed?

The ethical justifications given at the outset – social justice, security, freedom and solidarity – are powerful reasons for wanting a basic income system. But the urgency of needing it now reflects a perfect storm of factors that have created the basis for a remarkable coalition of supporters.

Most debate in Britain on social policy refers back to William Beveridge's epoch-defining report in 1942, which established the principles that would bring us the National Health Service (NHS) and the post-war system of social security that is now in tatters. But the type of economy and labour market of Beveridge's time differed sharply from current realities. We are living in an age of economic *uncertainty*, for which contributory insurance schemes are inappropriate or insufficient. Today a growing proportion of people are in the precariat, living bits-and-pieces lives, relying on low wages and incomes that are increasingly volatile and unpredictable and on inadequate and uncertain benefits in times of loss of earnings power.

It is often forgotten by social policy commentators that Beveridge advocated a minimum income floor, and even presumed it would be part of the post-war system. But this was never implemented, which was to prove a key limitation as the industrial society on which his system was based started to fade into British history.

When he wrote his report, Beveridge said it was a 'time for revolutions, not patching'. He was correct, since the old pre-war framework had broken down and was unable to deal with the Great Depression. He summarized what he believed to be the post-war challenge as the need to slay five giants – disease, idleness, ignorance, squalor and want. These giants remain, albeit in attenuated form. But today there are eight more giants stalking the land.

Slaying the eight modern giants

(1) *Inequality*

The first giant blocking the road to a Good Society is inequality. Britain is far more unequal today than in the 1970s and more unequal than any other major industrialized country barring the United States. The Gini coefficient – a summary measure of income inequality – has risen from under 0.25 in the late 1970s to 0.34 in 2017–18, a huge increase. However, according to the conventional statistics, this increase took place primarily in the 1980s under the Thatcher government. The Gini coefficient has hardly budged since the 1990s, leading many commentators to claim that wealth and income gaps have been broadly stable since then.[4] Yet other evidence indicates that the growth of inequality in recent years has been far greater than the conventional statistics suggest.

The Conservative government has repeatedly claimed that inequality has fallen on its watch. As the Secretary of State for Work and Pensions Amber Rudd proclaimed at the end of March 2018, 'Since we entered government in 2010, income inequality has fallen.' In the same month, her own department issued a report admitting that inequality had increased due to a rise in the earnings of high-paid workers and the continuing freeze on the level of benefits.[5]

In May 2019, when the Institute for Fiscal Studies (IFS) announced a five-year study of inequality led by Nobel Laureate Sir Angus Deaton, its report accompanying the launch also claimed that income inequality had been stable.[6] US-based Angus Deaton spoke at the launch as if the giant had not been growing for decades but was merely in danger of growing. He told the media, 'There are things where Britain is still doing a lot better [than the United States]. What we have to do is to make sure the UK is inoculated from some of the horrors that have happened in the US.' On cue, in response to the launch of the IFS review, the Treasury claimed, 'Our policies are highly redistributive. ... Income inequality is lower now than it was in 2010.'

The first reason for doubting this claim is the evidence of our own eyes. Destitution, homelessness and rough sleeping have soared since 2010, as anyone can see for themselves in the streets of Britain's towns and cities. Rough sleeping rose by 165% between 2010 and 2018, and the number of food banks rose from 29 to over 2,000.[7]

Child poverty has risen sharply. In 2018, over four million children were in households that were too poor to enable them to have a healthy diet, even though many of their parents had jobs.[8] Those families lacked money; the social security system was failing them. In a wealthy country like Britain, no child should be going to bed hungry, and for four million to be doing so is an indictment of the benefits system. The Resolution Foundation estimated that the roll-out of UC and other welfare cuts will increase the number of children in poverty to more than five million by 2020. Nearly 40% of all children will be living in poverty by 2021.

Poverty among working-age adults has also been rising since the 1990s.[9] It is commonly claimed that 'work is the best route out of poverty'. Yet today in Britain, of the more than 14 million people classified as living in poverty, 8 million or 58% have someone in the household in employment, up from 37% in 1995.[10] Some 2.8 million people are living in poverty despite having all adults in their household employed full-time.[11] Nearly three quarters of children in poverty have one or both parents in jobs, compared with about half in the 1990s. The fact is that a growing number of jobs do not enable people to escape from income poverty. Reforms in labour standards, minimum wages and collective bargaining could moderate this, but the pattern is likely to persist. Britain is not alone in this trend, but it has been among the worst.[12]

It is highly unlikely that, despite all these trends, there has been no increase in overall inequality. And it is worth highlighting some simple flaws in the statistics on which claims that there has been no such increase are based. Collected by the Department for Work and Pensions (DWP) in the form of the Family Resources Survey of households, these data have significant limitations.

In particular, they omit the top 3% of incomes. Omitting them in a narrative on inequality is equivalent to Hamlet without the Prince. According to other data, the income share of the top 1%, after tax and before housing costs, rose from 3% in the mid-1970s to about 8% in 2017, and this is likely to be a substantial underestimate due to under-recording of top incomes. The issues of non-response and misreporting of top incomes are very well known, and some components of income obtained by the rich are easily excluded, such as imputed rents and retained earnings in companies that increase wealth in the longer term.[13]

It is nevertheless clear that the very top has done rather well. In 2017–18, the UK had the dubious distinction of having the person with the world's highest salary. It happened to be a woman (raising the mean average for women relative to men rather misleadingly). She is the chief executive of BET365, who received (one baulks at the word 'earned') a salary of £220 million for the year, supplemented by dividends from her company of £45 million. In the previous year, her salary was a mere £199 million, implying an annual increase of 10%.

In 2018 the Swiss bank Credit Suisse reported that the ranks of the ultra-rich in Britain swelled by 400 in the 12 months to summer 2018, taking the number with wealth of over $50 million (£38 million) to nearly 4,670.[14] The bank said there were many more hovering just below that threshold. Reportedly the richest man in the country, with a self-revealed wealth of over £22 billion, Jim Ratcliffe (a Brexit advocate), just after receiving a knighthood, announced he was off to live in the tax haven of Monaco, so as to avoid paying tax.

It is not just the top 1% of incomes that is at issue here. The top 5% has also bounded ahead to take a growing share of total income.[15] The researchers in this study claimed that the relative stability of the Gini coefficient therefore implied that inequality had fallen 'across the large majority of the income distribution' over the previous decade. Even if true, which is moot, the same may have prevailed in France in the years before 1789; if attention had focused on just the middle-income groups, nobody would have predicted the revolution.[16]

Moreover, the analyses based on the DWP's household survey exclude not only the top 3% but also the bottom 3%.[17] While the top 3% have gained, the omission of the bottom 3% is also distorting. There are reasons for believing that their absolute and relative income has fallen. Indeed, if more of the lowest income earners have slipped into homelessness, which has grown enormously, they could have drifted out of the *household* survey altogether, lowering measured inequality artificially.[18]

In sum, the most-cited official figures exclude not only the super-rich (the top 0.1%) and the very rich (the top 3%) but also the homeless and the poorest 3% of households, conveniently excluded on the grounds that the data are unreliable. Since we know the incomes of the rich have raced ahead, while many of the poorest are excluded from the figures, it follows that the income gap between rich and poor has been widening.

The rise of rentier capitalism

There is a structural reason for the rise of the inequality giant: the income distribution system that prevailed in the post-1945 era has broken down irretrievably. This is a global phenomenon, not restricted just to Britain, even though it has been worsened in Britain by the inequalities of austerity. The gradual collapse in the income distribution system began with the adoption of what is now called 'neoliberalism' in the 1980s, led by Margaret Thatcher and Ronald Reagan and guided by a bunch of economists linked to the Mont Pelerin Society.

Neoliberalism may be characterized as the belief in open 'free' markets, defined by privatization, the sanctity of private property rights, free trade and minimal roles for protective labour regulations and collective bodies, which neoliberals see as distorting market forces. But, though preaching belief in free markets, neoliberalism actually ushered in an era dominated by finance with the most unfree market system ever envisaged, regulated in favour of corporations and rentiers. Ostensibly to attract capital, successive governments have cut taxes on profits and high incomes, and have increased subsidies to corporations and property owners, while cutting benefits and subsidies for lower-income groups.

The global economy has moved into what is best described as 'rentier capitalism', in which the economic returns to property – physical, financial and 'intellectual' – have jumped dramatically, while the returns to labour have dropped.[19] Rentier income is rising relative to both profits from production and income from labour. And workers are being deprived of the rental income gained by monopolistic firms – the extra profits they make from charging higher prices in an uncompetitive market. A recent study concluded that in the past three decades, the top 300 publicly quoted British companies reduced the extent to which they shared rental income with their workers.[20]

Rentier capitalism has produced the most defining feature of current income distribution. For much of the twentieth century, the share of national income going to profits and the share going to workers in the form of wages and benefits were roughly constant. In the post-1945 era, wages on average rose steadily and wage and salary differentials were modest. That ended in the 1970s. Since the 1980s, the labour share in national income has shrunk – from about 65% to around 55%, according to the Office for National Statistics (ONS) – and earnings differentials have widened.[21] In 2018, GDP was nearly 10% larger than its pre-crash peak, yet median earnings even in money terms were lower than in 2008.

Given globalization, the ongoing technological revolution and the hegemonic 'intellectual property rights' regime that Britain will be unable to change, it would require unprecedented – and most unlikely – international coordination to alter the current trends. The old income distribution system is not only broken but most unlikely to return. If we could just accept that, we could concentrate on building a new distribution system fit for the twenty-first century.

Within the context of a continuing flow of income away from labour, there has also been a systematic dismantling of the structure of 'social income' that moderated inequality in the preceding era. If we start with what has been happening to wages, we can see how the labour market is failing.[22]

Unlike profits, rent and dividends, wages in Britain have fallen or stagnated for many years. According to the International Labour Organization's *Global Wage Report 2018/19*, between 2008 and 2017 average real wages fell further in the UK than in any other advanced G20 country. The ONS reported that in 2018 average total pay including bonuses was £491 a week, £31 lower than a decade earlier. The Resolution Foundation has estimated that, whereas for many decades the average wage doubled every 29 years, now it may not double again before the end of the century, and then only if favourable circumstances hold.

There is also a lot of anecdotal data to suggest that many more people must do more work that is not paid. The precariat, in particular, must use more unpaid time doing activities that are work but not counted as such. And over a million workers are doing unpaid overtime hours. This means average hourly *wage rates* are lower than they appear. If, as is likely, it is lower-earning workers who are mainly affected, this in itself will have widened wage inequality.

Wage differentials have grown enormously. Earnings at the top have risen much faster than in the middle, and real earnings have fallen for lower-paid men.[23] For those in the bottom half of the income spectrum – most in the precariat – wages have fallen by more than average and can be expected to continue to lag behind those of the minority earning good salaries and receiving part of the rental income from the high and rising returns to capital and ownership of physical, financial and intellectual property.

Wages have stagnated in all industrialized countries, even where unions are much stronger than they are in Britain.[24] The country needs stronger unions with fresh ideas. But in a globalized economic system, particularly one characterized by rentier capitalism rather than free markets, the ability to raise real wages is limited.

Demographic changes have also worsened income inequality. Women's earnings have risen relative to men's. This should be good news, but partly reflects the decline in men's average real wages and a rise in male earnings inequality. As these trends have broadly offset each other, measured earnings inequality across *individuals* has not changed much. But low-wage men have lost out and have not benefited from women's rising incomes. High-earning women tend to link up with high-earning men, so the two trends combined have increased *household* earnings inequality.[25]

The young have lost relative to older citizens. This is partly because more young people have been entering the precariat, who have experienced volatile stagnant wages and intermittent earnings, exposed to zero-hours contracts and so on.[26] And it is partly because of the government's 'triple-lock' policy of protecting pensioners' incomes, so that workers have lost income relative to pensioners.[27] Removing pensioners from the calculations makes clear how the production and employment system is fostering more inequality.

Wages are only part of workers' social income. In the post-war era, non-wage enterprise-based benefits – such as paid holidays and paid medical leave, subsidized transport and food, annual bonuses, premium pay for unsocial hours and occupational defined-benefit pensions – rose as a share of total compensation. As many of these were paid equally to all workers, they tended to moderate earnings inequality. But with the growth of the precariat fewer workers, young and old, have access to such benefits, and many firms have quietly converted them into money wages, giving a false impression of income growth.[28]

Meanwhile, those still in the salariat – on a stable contracted salary – have gained more in such benefits, the value of which has been elevated by tax policies. What has happened to non-wage benefits is a largely unmeasured aspect of growing income inequality in Britain, particularly between the precariat and the salariat. However, it is likely that the trend is similar to that in the United States. According to the official Bureau of Economic Analysis, the lowest 10% of US wage earners saw non-wage benefits fall by about 2% in real terms between 2009 and 2018, while the top 10% enjoyed a rise of 17%.[29]

Another sign of the failing distribution system is that by 2019 one in every three working-age households was receiving state benefits of one kind or another, including tax credits. Traditionally, state benefits, or welfare, have moderated inequality, although by less than most commentators have presumed. In recent years, however, benefit cuts have put that into reverse.[30] Their real value has been reduced, they have been made more difficult to claim and a vicious sanctions regime has deprived people of benefits to which they are entitled. The disastrous introduction of UC, discussed later, has impoverished many previously living on the edge. Rising costs of essentials, especially for rented housing, have also slashed living standards. And although UK public social spending as a percentage of GDP, at 20.6% in 2018, is already lower than the European Union average, and compares with 31.2% in France and 25.1% in Germany, the government was planning further cuts over the next few years.

Another unappreciated factor in the growth of inequality is the plunder of the commons, accelerated by the austerity regime and systemic privatization. This has led to deepening and perceptible 'social income' inequality, depriving people of free or subsidized public services and amenities on which many low-income households depend, including parks, libraries, leisure centres, bus services, playgrounds and youth clubs, as well as health, education and care services.[31]

Finally, the tax system has become less progressive. According to the ONS, in recent years 'overall, taxes had a negligible effect on income inequality'.[32] Traditionally, taxes have tended to reduce inequality, but changes introduced since 2010 have reversed that. Even the rise in personal tax allowances has been regressive, as have large cuts in corporation tax.

More than 100 tax reliefs have been added to the edifice of over 1,150, amounting to a huge subsidy to the wealthy. For instance, Entrepreneurs' Relief has reduced the tax paid by affluent entrepreneurs, while employer National Insurance tax breaks for pension contributions have benefited the salariat. Overall, the British tax system is less effective at reducing inequality than the tax systems of most EU countries, including France, Germany and Italy.[33]

Now we come to the biggest weakness in the claims that inequality has not increased. Wealth has risen faster than income. Wealth inequality in the UK is much greater than income inequality and is well above the OECD average. As private wealth has risen from about three times GDP in the 1960s and 1970s to nearly seven times now,[34] the shift from income to wealth must have raised total inequality, even if wealth inequality and income inequality had stayed the same, which is doubtful. So, wealth and income inequality combined must have increased.

Since the Big Bang liberalization of financial markets under the Thatcher government, Britain has become much more reliant on the financial sector. Its assets now amount to over 300% of GDP, up from about 100% in the 1970s, while net public wealth has declined, partly due to a transfer of public to private wealth.[35] And the concentration of private wealth has increased. While overall wealth has boomed, the poorest fifth of households have experienced a decline in wealth in real terms.[36]

Wealth inequality is also increasingly underestimated, partly because it has been easier to squirrel away financial wealth in tax havens and in fancy financial instruments beyond the reach of regulators and tax collectors. Globally, hidden financial wealth may account for 10% of the world's GDP, and such is the scope for wealthy people in Britain to hide theirs that the UK is much above average in this respect.[37]

A conscientious study of international tax evasion and avoidance showed that UK unrecorded offshore wealth has grown rapidly since the 1980s and by much more than recorded onshore wealth.[38] It is almost double what it is in other countries, amounting to almost 20% of GDP. That long-term trend has concealed the extent of the growth of wealth and income inequality.

To compound the inequality, over 60% of all wealth in the UK has been inherited, a proportion that is rising. In other words, it is unearned and could be called 'something for nothing'. The 'something-for-nothing' economy has done rather well; most of the rise in wealth has had nothing to do with work. That should be borne in mind when we hear politicians criticize state benefits as 'something for nothing'.

The growth of wealth inequality is accentuated by ageing, since the elderly have benefited disproportionately from property price rises. Wealth has been boosted by the sustained rise in the value of land, which now accounts for 51% of the UK's measured net worth, higher than in any other big industrialized country. This has fuelled the rise in property prices and the value of property inheritance.

In his 2015 Budget, George Osborne increased the tax-free allowance for inheritance tax in stages from an already generous £650,000 for a couple, which from 2020 will enable the tax-free inheritance of a property worth up to £1 million. This represents a gift worth £140,000 to wealthy people – removal of a 40% tax on £350,000. In the light of such giveaways to the affluent, how can anybody say, as the economics editor of the *Financial Times* has argued, that in the austerity era 'we have all been in it together'?[39]

The inheritance bonus is linked to the rising inter-generational transfer of inequality. The so-called 'baby boomer' generation born after the Second World War has done well out of the property market and is now beginning to fade out. The Resolution Foundation found that 83% of those in their twenties and thirties who own homes have parents who own homes, whereas almost half of the younger generation who do not own a home have parents who do not own one either.[40] So, living standard inequality is accentuated by the transmission of wealth.

Britain is now the most unequal of any rich industrialized economy except the United States.[41] But the adverse trends are global; inequality is growing everywhere.

The giant represented by rising inequality is causing disquiet even among the winners in the rentier economy. The more thoughtful among them realize they have been winning too much, and that such an unbalanced system is economically, morally and politically unsustainable. They are expecting to have to make concessions. Some are openly saying so.

The existing inequalities are unjustified on grounds of social justice, and there is no evidence that they have any economic benefit, let alone social benefit. Instead, the huge and growing inequality of wealth has provided a privileged minority with a lot of 'something-for-nothing'. Accusations that a basic income would be something-for-nothing are thus hypocritical. And, in any case, a basic income would not be something-for-nothing. It would be providing people with something in order to become more active and social citizens.

Given the emergence of rentier capitalism and the growth of multiple forms of inequality, a sensible practical strategy would be to recycle much of the rental income, from the few to the many, and the best way of doing that would be through basic income in the form of common dividends. Reinforcing this proposal is research showing that reducing inequality is a more effective way of reducing absolute poverty than chasing higher economic growth.

A basic income system would compensate commoners for loss of the commons, which deprives them of their birth-rights. It would compensate those who do not have the ability to make money or inherit property, and it would compensate those hit by the inequality implicit in ecological developments (discussed later). If properly designed, a basic income would reduce inequality and do so without distorting the economy.

When considering the scope for moderating inequality via basic income or common dividends, we should bear in mind what even modest payments would do. Low-income families need a third more income than a decade ago to have a socially acceptable ('minimum income') standard of living, according to research by the Joseph Rowntree Foundation. To put that into perspective, a lone parent employed full-time on the minimum wage would be short of that acceptable minimum by £70 a week. So, a basic income of that amount would enable a lone parent to move out of poverty, and even one as low as £50 would go a long way to that end.

(2)   *Insecurity*

Alongside the giant of inequality is the giant of economic insecurity. There has always been insecurity in society, and it has long been known that it has deleterious consequences for individuals, families and communities. But the welfare state that took shape after the Second World War was supposed to reduce social and economic insecurity.

The essence of the Beveridge model was that the state would limit the risk of adverse events – shocks – and provide contributions-based insurance (mainly paid by employers) to enable people and families to cope with them better and to recover from them sooner and more easily. The main shocks, known as contingency risks, were unemployment, illness, accident, disability, frailty and old age.

The trouble started when the contributory principle frayed: entitlement to benefits had to be extended to people who were not in a position to pay contributions, or have them paid on their behalf, and more people were unable to build up adequate contribution records. As increasing numbers of those in jobs suffered from poverty and income volatility, so-called in-work benefits were expanded. At every point, decisions had to be made about who 'deserved' to receive benefits and who did not. The result of these developments was greater complexity and more arbitrary decisions by bureaucrats. The social security system itself became a zone of insecurity.

At the same time, the nature of people's insecurity has changed. Modern insecurity is characterized by chronic *uncertainty*. Economists differentiate between risk and uncertainty. With risks you can calculate the probability of adverse or favourable outcomes and develop an insurance strategy based on probabilities. National or social insurance schemes could pool risks, with those facing low probabilities of an adverse event subsidizing those facing higher probabilities. With uncertainty, you just do not know. There are 'unknown unknowns'. No actuarial calculation of probabilities can be made and so it is hard to develop a social insurance system as an adequate response.

Uncertainty dominates twenty-first-century insecurity. You can be adversely affected by events that take place on the other side of the world, by elections elsewhere, by natural disasters, by trade shifts that reflect a technological breakthrough somewhere or other and so on. Who is hurt and who gains is almost random, except that those with more resources do not seem to be hit and often seem to gain from such misfortunes.

Insecurity is chronic. Today, regardless of their employment contract, many more people in jobs are afraid of losing or expect to lose their jobs. More people feel insecure about their home; more feel insecure about their personal relationships; and more of those feeling insecure act inadvertently in ways that make all that worse.[42]

Basic security is a superior public good. It is a basic human need, and one person having it does not deprive others of having it. What makes it a superior public good is that others having it improves one's own basic security. Social policy should be judged by whether or not it provides basic security, and basic income does just that. It would reduce economic uncertainty, and would strengthen personal, family and community resilience. It would do so much better than a negative income tax (NIT), which is sometimes proposed as an alternative, since with a NIT there is no *a priori* knowledge of how much a potential recipient would receive, and the amount would tend to fluctuate in value, as well as being complex to calculate and administer.

Means-tested and behaviour-tested social assistance that currently define Britain's welfare system intensify personal and family insecurity, lowering the value of any benefits on offer. No government has thus far given basic security the priority it deserves. Moving towards a basic income system would change that.

(3) *Debt*

The financial crash in 2007–08 was blamed by the Conservatives on 'public indebtedness', which they used to justify their later austerity strategy. In fact, it was high *private* debt that created the conditions for the crash, and *not* public debt.

As Rickard Nyman and Paul Ormerod concluded from an exhaustive review of the data, 'The evidence suggests quite clearly that public sector debt played no causal role in generating the Great Recession. In contrast, the ratio of private sector debt to GDP does appear to have played a significant role, especially in the UK.'[43]

Although down from peak post-crash levels, the ratio of household debt to GDP remains high at around 90%, well above the 50% EU average. And borrowing far exceeds savings, by a bigger margin than in any other OECD country.[44] Consumption has grown faster than incomes, as people have tried to maintain living standards in the face of low or stagnant wages.

The private debt crisis can be seen as reflecting the end of the Faustian bargain of the tax credit era, when rising tax credits allowed consumption to run ahead of earned incomes. A related interpretation is that what has happened is a failure of disposable income to keep up with GDP. More debt has filled the gap. The trend is unsustainable.

Consumer borrowing reached £213 billion in 2018 and has been rising much faster than wages. By mid-2018, unsecured household debt was higher than at any time on record, with households on average spending £900 more than they received in income during 2017. The Trades Union Congress has estimated that unsecured household debt, including student loans, averaged £15,400 in 2018, and could rise to £19,000 in 2022 if current trends continue. Even excluding student loans, average unsecured household debt was over £11,000 in 2018, still a record. Some 8.3 million people were struggling with 'problem debt' arising from unsecured consumer credit. Debt has also been exacerbated by the four-year freeze on Local Housing Allowances, used to calculate Housing Benefit for private tenants. Almost everywhere debt has been rising.

For instance, in Fife rent arrears by council tenants were rising by £120,000 a month in 2018, and in October that year were standing at over £8 million, from a council house population of about 30,000. Most of those in arrears were on Universal Credit. As elsewhere in Britain, the debt was further reducing the council's capacity to finance social care and other essentials.

Private debt has a wider cost for society. The National Audit Office (NAO) estimated that the economy loses £900 million a year from the adverse effects of private debt, due to the resultant ill-health from stress and anxiety and increased use of the NHS, increased crime, more depression and lower productivity, compounded by the government's debt collection practices.[45] There is also 'concealed debt' in the form of unpaid utility bills, missing council tax payments and alleged overpaid benefits, amounting to some £19 billion.[46]

Debt is worsened by erratic earnings. The Resolution Foundation found that nearly three quarters of workers with steady jobs have unsteady incomes, with extreme monthly volatility the overwhelming norm for low-paid workers. Most could not make savings to smooth the volatility, instead experiencing more stress and rising debt. Routinely running out of money for short periods, due to fluctuating earnings, causes people to skip medications and resort to payday lenders.[47]

A particularly venomous way by which debt has been multiplied to the point of crushing people has been the use of aggressive debt collection methods by local authorities. Under the rules, if someone falls behind on their monthly council tax, after two weeks they become liable for the rest of the annual tax bill, and two fees are added, court costs and bailiff fees. The outcome is that an initial debt of £167 (the average council tax payment) can multiply to over £2,000 in just nine weeks.[48] As a result of this system, council tax debt grew by 30% between 2010 and 2018, when it stood at over £3 billion, excluding fees. One in every 10 households was behind with their council tax.

Debt is a mechanism for hidden inequality. While middle-income and upper-income citizens can use debt in the form of low-cost mortgages to have a comfortable lifestyle and an asset of rising real value, reliance on unsecured debt leads to a much higher cost of living for those on low incomes. Missed or delayed payments result in a low credit rating that means they can only obtain high-cost loans and may be refused access to social housing run by housing associations, supposedly operating to help low-income people. Having debt may thus make a person not only more likely to become homeless but also less likely to obtain a home when they are homeless.[49]

Debt is systemic in modern Britain, and its reduction must become a key aspect of social policy. A basic income would not eradicate debt, but it would help to limit involuntary debt; it would give individuals and families more control of their finances, knowing that at least a modest amount was coming in every month without fail. The evidence from pilots elsewhere shows that even a small basic income results in less indebtedness.

Unless something is done to arrest its growth, debt will almost inevitably precipitate another financial crisis. As was shown after the financial crisis of 2007–08, stopgap policies introduced in haste will be inefficient and sluggish, leaving many people needlessly and permanently scarred. A basic income system would impart greater resilience in the face of such predictable crises, to individuals and to the country.

(4)   *Stress*

Our society is confronted by a pandemic of stress, another giant that is an indictment of a wealthy country. Stress is debilitating, reduces the capacity to think clearly and long term and has contributed to a rise in morbidity involving more physical and mental ill-health, including a rise in suicides and suicidal tendencies. It has been exacerbated by insecurity, debt and inequality.[50]

More people report feeling out of control of their lives, feeling their time is squeezed and that demands on them are incessant. In 2017–18, stress was found to be responsible for 44% of all work-related ill-health cases and 57% of all working days lost to ill-health.[51] A quarter of all adults were suffering from stress-related long-term ill-health.[52] The perceived threat of destitution has also been linked to physical ill-health.

Chronic psychological stress is linked to greater risk of depression, heart disease, diabetes, autoimmune diseases, upper respiratory infections and poorer wound healing.[53] To put the failure to address this in perspective, in 2018 an authoritative study showed that the UK was one of only two OECD countries (the other being the United States) in which average life expectancy was declining. Since 2010, the mortality rate among men aged 45 to 54 has been rising steadily, despite declines in deaths from cancer and heart disease. So-called deaths of despair have been rising among both men and women, but more so for men.[54]

Stress is compounded by money worries and anxiety about fulfilling conditions for means-tested and behaviour-tested benefits. The Adult Psychiatric Morbidity Survey carried out for the NHS found that 43% of disabled people receiving Employment Support Allowance (ESA) had attempted suicide at some point in their lives, compared with 7% of other adults, while two-thirds had had suicidal thoughts.[55]

Care should have been taken to avoid adding to the stress they were bearing. Nothing was done. In late 2018, the government implicitly recognized the crisis by making the 'mental health minister' also the 'minister for suicide prevention', surely a reflection of an unfolding social tragedy. The ESA policy had strengthened suicidal tendencies, and yet the government persisted with it.

Psychologists have shown that 'resource scarcity deprives individuals of fluid intelligence, compounding the disadvantage conferred by lives of poverty'.[56] Income insecurity causes stress and narrows 'mental bandwidth', leading to a lowering of short-term IQ and more focus on short-term choices rather than longer-term strategic thinking.[57] It is unfair to judge stressed-out people for making poor decisions if the economic system beyond their control is largely responsible for the psychological conditions.

The threat of sanctions or withdrawal of welfare benefits also intensifies stress for recipients. It has even led to what the Activity

Alliance has dubbed an 'activity trap' – reduced activity by disabled people who fear that evidence of activity, even going out of the house, will be seen by the authorities as a reason to take their benefits away.[58] One claimant reported to her GP, 'You want to prove to the state that you're as ill and disabled and incapable as you possibly can; otherwise, your kids might starve.' This might be dismissed as extreme, but it would be hard to deny that a zone of conflict has been created.

Most NHS mental health trusts in England have reported that benefit changes and the roll-out of Universal Credit have increased mental ill-health and the demand for medical services.[59] Uncertainty plays on the mind.

A basic income could be expected to reduce the incidence and intensity of stress, partly by improving people's sense of control of their time. The opposite is the case with existing social assistance policies. Past and ongoing pilots elsewhere have shown that basic income tends to reduce stress and thus improve health, reducing healthcare costs and raising productivity, at both individual and community levels.

A remarkable finding from the three-year Mincome (quasi-basic income) experiment in Manitoba, Canada, in the 1970s (see Appendix A), was that resort to healthcare services dropped by 8%, due to self-reported improvements in health. Critics of basic income who emphasize affordability rarely take account of the likely reduction in other public costs that would come with its introduction.

In a basic income experiment in Ontario, Canada, launched in 2017 but abruptly terminated by a right-wing provincial government on taking office, an analysis of the data gathered in the first year found that 88% of basic income recipients reported feeling less stressed. And in Finland, an official analysis of the first year of a two-year basic income pilot found that the incidence of depression among recipients had fallen by 37%. In other pilots, the payment of individual basic incomes has been associated with a reduction in domestic violence. Such findings imply that even modest basic income payments would have some social value beyond their impact on poverty and inequality.

(5) *Precarity*

Millions of people are living bits-and-pieces lives that go beyond issues of insecurity and stress. They feel that they are unable to develop themselves, have no occupational identity or narrative to give to their lives and must do a lot of work that is not recognized or remunerated. They are the precariat.[60]

Perhaps worst of all, they are, and feel like, *supplicants*: they must ask for favours, for permission, for help, which if not granted threaten their ability to function. The original Latin meaning of precariousness was 'to obtain by prayer'. That is what being in the precariat is like; they are dependent on others' goodwill. This is undignified, potentially traumatizing and puts people on the road to losing the ordinary rights of citizenship, exemplified by the increasingly discretionary character of welfare benefits. A case in point was the government's closure of the national Social Fund, which made one-off payments for exceptional needs such as replacing a fridge or a bed, and the slow evaporation of funding for the devolved welfare assistance schemes that replaced it. Applicants must now plead for assistance. But at least 28 local authorities have closed their schemes altogether, through lack of funding, while others have shredded theirs.

More people are drifting down from the precariat into destitution, relying on food banks and other forms of discretionary charity. There was a fortyfold increase in the use of food banks between 2008 and 2017; in 2018, the Trussell Trust recorded a 52% year-on-year increase in the number of three-day emergency food packages distributed.

In December 2018, several Conservative MPs were shown taking photographs of themselves handing food donations to new food banks. Each said exactly what their colleagues were saying in other constituencies, suggesting that the actions were coordinated, while the smiles suggested that they thought this was a policy achievement rather than a reflection of policy failure. The photographs went viral on social media. Sarcastic comments did too.

Food banks have been opening all over the country. The city of Belfast is fairly typical. In 2012, there was just one food bank; in 2018, there were 17. Britain is drifting into a state of supplicants. There are fewer and weaker barriers to crashing out.

Social policy should be judged by whether it reduces or intensifies precarity. A basic income would increase people's sense of agency, of feeling more in control and thus able to exert more freedom of choice. Freedom should matter just as much for the disadvantaged as for everybody else.

Instead, policy trends have substantially increased the extent of precariousness, by making many more people dependent on satisfying state and private bureaucrats. The government has used the power of the state to *control* disadvantaged people's lives; a progressive government should use the power of the state to *empower* disadvantaged people.

In this respect, a basic income would do something that, however well intentioned, paternalist social policy would not do. As envisaged in the proposal for 'universal basic services' (discussed in Appendix C), subsidizing specific services, as opposed to giving people cash, presumes those services are what people want and that they can be provided to everybody needing them.

There is no contradiction between having quasi-universal basic services and a basic income. They are not mutually exclusive. They address different needs. But having cash in the form of a guaranteed basic income would enhance freedom of choice and the more important republican freedom, while being more empowering and more transformative.

(6) *The robot advance*

One relatively new justification for a basic income is the threat to jobs posed by robots and Artificial Intelligence (AI). The Bank of England, the OECD and the McKinsey Global Institute are among those predicting the disappearance of huge numbers of jobs over the next two decades.[61] Elon Musk, one of several very wealthy and successful entrepreneurs who have made similar statements, has concluded that a basic income is a necessary policy for a fast-approaching future in which 'there will be fewer and fewer jobs that a robot cannot do better'.

There are reasons for scepticism about the more apocalyptic forecasts. Some, such as the World Economic Forum, have even predicted that AI will increase the number of jobs.[62] Perhaps. But what is certain is that the ongoing technological revolution is and will be increasingly *disruptive* and is already contributing to the economic uncertainty of modern life in Britain and elsewhere.

The technological revolution is accentuating the growing inequality. High-paying but automatable jobs may be more threatened than low-skilled, low-wage jobs such as care work or cleaning.[63] The International Monetary Fund (IMF) has joined those predicting that robots will raise production but lower wages. Robot owners will gain, workers will lose. As the IMF concluded, 'Our main results are surprisingly robust: automation is good for growth and bad for equality.'[64] Others have found that automation has been driving down the share of income going to labour.[65]

There is also a spreading view that robots and AI threaten to make more people *irrelevant* in the production process and in society, with a loss of control over how they can live. But the main feeling is that massive change is coming, for better or for worse. And we are still in the early 'installation' phase of a technological revolution that will roll out over decades.[66] The message should be clear. We need to have in place a distribution system that will ensure everybody in society shares in the economic gains from automation and AI.

The social protection system should be designed to respond to disruptive and even unpredictable changes resulting from technological trends. A basic income would be a form of preparatory insurance, giving everybody a greater sense of basic security against the understandable public fear of human displacement. Once in place, the basic income could be raised if anything like the dire predictions turned out to be true. Having a basic income system would also encourage people to welcome technological advances, avoiding the perfectly respectable Luddite reaction of the early nineteenth century when workers objected to mechanization because they were forced to lose and not share the gains.

The assumed threat to jobs from automation has also led to calls to cut the working week to share jobs around and improve work-life balance. One proponent has even suggested that the target should be a 21-hour week. This policy might be desirable in a utopia, but it would be deeply impractical. It would be particularly inappropriate for a labour market based on flexible labour relations. It would be impossible and surely undesirable to stop people wanting to work longer than whatever duration was specified as the maximum.

A lesson from France, where such a policy was pursued for years, is that the imposition of the 35-hour working week was followed by an *increase* in average working time to over 35 hours. Nobody should be required or expected to work in a job longer than 38 or 40 hours a week. But everybody should be enabled to choose how many or how few hours they wish to put in. A basic income would enable more people to do fewer hours of paid work a week if they wished. We would be likely to see a shorter working week on average, without trying to force people into it.

One interesting study suggests that British workers should put in no more than nine hours a week in order to reduce carbon emissions to the level required to avoid more than 2°C global heating.[67] This would require wage rates to rise considerably to maintain living standards or the introduction of a basic income. The latter would encourage forms of work that are not resource-depleting and energy-using labour.

(7) *Extinction*

The ecological crisis is an existential issue for humanity and the planet, and a giant confronting every individual in the country. Drastic measures are required to arrest global warming, combat pollution and revive ecosystems.

Too many of us disregard what is happening unless it hits us personally or hits someone close to us. This myopic perspective must change. Late 2018 saw the beginning of a movement with the deliberately alarming name of 'Extinction Rebellion'. This has the potential to become a powerful twenty-first-century movement and deserves support.

In Britain and around the world, children in particular are suffering life-threatening illness from toxic air linked to transport using fossil fuels. Burning fossil fuels has been termed 'the world's most significant threat to children's health'[68] while 'long-term exposure to air pollution impedes cognitive performance in verbal and math tests'.[69] Air pollution is now the single biggest threat to human health, inducing not only physical but mental illness and accelerating dementia.[70] And it is a source of inequality, since low-income communities are more exposed. In Britain, the Royal College of Physicians has estimated that air pollution results in 40,000 premature deaths each year,[71] and research published in the *European Heart Journal* estimated that it cuts average life expectancy by one and a half years.[72]

Fossil fuels are also the main source of greenhouse gas emissions. The perils of rapid climate change have become only too clear, with Britain too facing disruption of weather patterns, droughts, floods and the threat of rising sea levels. All mainstream political parties have committed to the country's pledge under the Paris Agreement of 2015 to slash CO_2 emissions by 2030. But existing policies fall far short of what is needed to honour our national pledge.

Moreover, in 2018, a report by the Intergovernmental Panel on Climate Change (IPCC) showed that to avoid massive and dangerous environmental destruction the world should be aiming to limit the rise in global temperatures to 1.5°C, rather than the 2°C targeted by the Paris Agreement. Yet, without urgent and decisive action, we will hit the critical 1.5°C temperature rise from pre-industrial levels by 2030. Rapid decarbonization is the only way forward.

One necessary measure is a substantial increase in carbon taxes. A statement issued at the UN Climate Summit in Poland in December 2018 by a powerful group of multinational investment funds managing $32 trillion of investors' money called for 'meaningful' taxes on carbon and an end to fossil fuel subsidies. According to calculations by Schroders, one of the signatories, failure to keep the rise in global temperatures to 2°C would cause long-term economic damage on three or four times the scale of the 2007–08 financial crash.[73]

A consensus is building. Research by the IMF has shown that a modest levy or tax on CO_2 emissions, of about £50 per tonne, would raise twice as much revenue as the conventional cap-and-trade approach, equivalent to as much as 2% of GDP. That would be 50% more effective in cutting greenhouse gases, enabling Britain to come close to meeting its Paris Agreement pledge.[74] It is imperative that we move in that direction.

There are two problems: taxes are unpopular and a carbon tax by itself would be regressive, since it would take a higher proportion of income from poorer households. President Macron in France has found that raising fuel tax without complementary measures can bring social strife and political instability. But experience in Canada and Switzerland shows that those problems can be overcome if the revenue gained from the carbon tax, or much of it, is then paid out as a dividend to everybody. In Switzerland, every household receives a dividend from the carbon levy as a rebate on their compulsory annual health insurance premiums. About two-thirds of the revenue raised from the levy is distributed, mainly going to households.

In Canada, the Liberal government plans to introduce an even higher fuel tax than Macron tried in France. However, the measure has popular support because it will be combined with the return of much of the revenue raised as dividends paid to everybody. The new federal scheme will rebate 90% of the revenues back to individual households, 70% of which will gain more from the rebate than they will pay in higher fuel prices. Households will receive hundreds of dollars a year in dividends, which will tend to reduce economic insecurity and inequality.[75] In Ireland, the Taoiseach in January 2019 endorsed a carbon tax with all funds raised to go in direct cash dividends. Something similar should be done in Britain.

Reinforcing the case for doing so, an American study found that, whereas a levy on CO_2 emissions would be regressive if used to cut personal income tax, it would be progressive, benefiting nearly all the bottom half of the population, if the receipts were recycled as universal lump-sum payments.[76] It would be even better if the receipts were placed in a national Commons Fund, from which quasi-universal dividends, a form of basic income, could be paid. Another study by an international group of social scientists also concluded that a carbon levy would be popular if combined with payment of dividends.[77]

We are facing an ecological disaster of catastrophic proportions unless we drastically alter the way we live and our reliance on economic growth to raise living standards. And since a disproportionate share of economic growth is now going to a minority at the top of the income spectrum, a higher rate of GDP growth is needed to reduce poverty. But more growth means more resource depletion, more greenhouse gas emissions and more pollution of all kinds. Greens advocate 'de-growth'. There is considerable merit in that position, but it would be a hard sell politically, since it would risk misinterpretation as telling voters they should expect a decline in living standards.

A better approach would be to recalibrate what is meant by growth, giving value to environmental indicators and forms of work that are not counted in GDP, perhaps using a 'genuine progress indicator', as some have proposed.[78]

One other change is vital. We must overcome the arbitrary distinction between 'work' and 'non-work' and give as much if not more value to forms of work that are not paid labour – care work, community work, work on improving our capabilities and so on. The ONS has estimated that unpaid housework, childcare and eldercare, overwhelmingly undertaken by women, are worth £1.24 trillion a year, almost £19,000 per person. This is greater than the £1.04 trillion contributed by all the UK's non-financial sectors.[79] Excluding this unpaid work from measures of national income not only results in a systematic underestimate of our national income but understates growth, since the value of such work has been rising.

This is fundamentally a feminist issue; the invisibility of work that is not labour has been a way of diminishing the contribution that women make to economic and social life. If we could escape from thinking that only paid labour counts as work to be rewarded, then society would give care work its true value. A basic income would encourage more of us to do more unpaid care and voluntary work, a desirable shift in our behaviour that would have desirable ecological outcomes as well. A basic income would be a way of ensuring we can all make better choices between forms of work and labour.

The onrushing ecological crisis may come to be regarded as the decisive justification for a basic income system. Ecological taxes and levies are needed to curb pollution, global warming and the plunder of the commons on which we all depend. But because some of those levies would be regressive, increasing inequalities, they will need to be matched by dividends paid equally to everybody.

This is not even a left-versus-right issue. It is attracting support from across the political spectrum, as evidenced by open support in a *Wall Street Journal* op-ed signed by a broad cross section of Democrats and Republicans and 27 Nobel-Prize-winning economists.[80] Carbon dividends represent a strong moral and politically practical justification for basic income. But Britain could go further than the good Canadian example, by recycling revenue not only from a carbon tax but from levies on all forms of pollution and intrusions into the commons.

(8) *Populism and neo-fascism*

The final giant is the rise of right-wing populism, epitomized by the election of Donald Trump as US president in November 2016, and by the spread of populist parties across Europe, where over a quarter of the electorate now support populist politicians, according to recent research. The definition of populism is vague, but most populists support aggressive nationalism, anti-migration posturing, hostility to mainstream politics of the centre left and centre right and a willingness to tolerate or openly support authoritarianism and anti-democratic policies.

In Britain, a national opinion poll carried out by the Hansard Society in early 2019 found disturbingly high support for political leadership prepared to disregard democratic norms, including 54%

support for the proposition 'Britain needs a strong leader willing to break the rules'. Democracy and the rule of law are under threat from the people themselves.

A major reason for the growing support for right-wing populism, or neo-fascism, is the toxic combination of chronic insecurity and precarity. A revealing survey in France and Germany found that people had turned to the far right because they felt devalued as citizens in the economy. It is not too fanciful to suggest that a basic income system, by lessening insecurity, precarity, debt and inequality, would arrest the drift to populism. People would feel more valued, have a bigger stake in the economic and political system, and see that government was not indifferent to the blatant inequalities they now observe around them.

A series of psychological experiments showed that people who were provided with basic income became more tolerant of 'strangers' and more cooperative in general.[81] In short, people with basic security are more likely to be responsible citizens.

We may conclude that a basic income and an income distribution system in which it is an anchor would help to weaken the threat posed by all eight of the modern giants blocking our route to a Good Society. A basic income would also help deal with Beveridge's five original giants. Critics of basic income should ponder whether any alternative social policy could confront the modern giants so effectively. And they should cease to regard basic income as solely a response to one issue, such as poverty or automation.

2

The immorality of Universal Credit

The construction of the welfare state was one of the great achievements of progressive governments in the twentieth century. However, reforms in the past four decades have weakened its moderating effect on inequality and contributed to increased insecurity, private debt, stress and precarity. By putting overwhelming emphasis on employment, including jobs that are resource-depleting, the present system disregards the ecological crisis. And its divisiveness and its impact on insecurity have been a factor in the growth of support for populist politics and the erosion of social solidarity.

These are strong claims. But the evidence in all respects is also strong. The problems started with decisions in the 1980s and 1990s to combine flexible labour markets, which in themselves increased economic insecurity, with a shift to greater reliance on means-testing. Means-testing is intended to target state benefits on those most in need, designated as 'the poor'. On the face of it, this sounds reasonable. But it involves 'tests' to determine who is poor and who is not, which is where the problems arise.

The first problem stems from the desire to exclude people deemed to have become poor by choice, because they are allegedly lazy or unreasonable. This requires use of 'behaviour tests' and 'attitude tests', which are inevitably arbitrary to some extent, as well as expensive to administer. They involve a large cumbersome bureaucracy prone to making numerous errors, however well intentioned the bureaucrats might be. There is vast evidence, from Britain and from every other country that has extended means-testing, that the errors are huge and inequitable.

The second problem is the creation of poverty traps. Going from receipt of a means-tested benefit into a job paying an above-poverty wage leads automatically to loss of benefits. This might not matter much if benefits were decent and if all jobs paid good wages and were full-time and stable. But in a flexible modern, service-oriented labour market, that is not the case. The sort of wages and jobs that someone on benefit could expect to obtain are low and uncertain. As successive governments have admitted, someone going from benefits into a low-paid job faces in effect a marginal tax rate of over 80%.

The poverty trap creates a moral hazard, because it acts as a disincentive to doing what someone would otherwise wish to do, in this case taking a job; it also creates an 'immoral' hazard: because people gain so little and lose so much, they may be tempted to enter the 'black economy', not declaring work they are doing, and thus risk losing entitlement to certain benefits and even prosecution.

And the poverty trap is worsened by the precarity trap. People do not obtain benefits immediately they become entitled to them and, particularly because of the deliberate delays introduced under Universal Credit, may wait many weeks. If and when they eventually do obtain benefits and are subsequently offered a short-term job, or one likely to last only a short time, they would be foolish to take it. Not only would they gain little extra, but they would face the prospect of soon being back in the queue waiting to renew benefits, perhaps without any income for several months. They would actually penalize themselves by taking a short-term job. This is grossly unfair and impoverishing.

The third problem is the requirement to apply for benefits and prove need. This is shaming, undignified, often costly, time-consuming and an implicit admission of personal inadequacy. It is potentially and often stigmatizing in the eyes of family, friends, neighbours and potential future employers. Some designers of means-tested, behaviour-tested conditional schemes explicitly want receipt of benefit to be shaming, so as to reduce claims and 'save' money. The Treasury even factors non-take-up into its forecasts of annual expenditure on welfare benefits, assuming that only a proportion of those entitled will claim or receive them.

Decades of research in many countries, including Britain, have shown, over and over again, that means-tested social assistance schemes invariably involve high exclusion errors, that is, a high share of those entitled to benefits do not receive them. Across all European Union countries, only about 60% of benefits to which people are entitled are claimed or obtained.[1] It is not just a British phenomenon; it is intrinsic to means-tested schemes in general.

Official estimates of non-take-up, which may be underestimates, show that in 2018 about 40% of households entitled to Pension Credit were not receiving it, 20% of those entitled to Housing Benefit were not receiving it, 44% of those entitled to Jobseeker's Allowance (JSA) did not receive it (a share that was rising) and half a million families with a disabled member entitled to Employment Support Allowance (ESA) were not receiving it. This does not mean those who are not claiming or receiving benefits do not need them. Many people will be just ashamed, or fear stigmatization, or will not know how to apply or how to navigate the rules.

In 2010, in a move ostensibly intended to simplify the welfare system, the Coalition government launched Universal Credit (UC), an ambitious reform that integrates six means-tested benefits, though with tougher conditions attached. Introduced by a driven secretary of state (and former leader of the Conservative Party), the scheme has been an unmitigated disaster.

The design and unrolling of UC have been beset by problems and delays. Originally planned to be up and running by 2017, as of early 2019, when a panicked just-appointed secretary of state announced a pause to the roll-out for existing benefit recipients, it was already running six years behind schedule.

UC could be described as the biggest single extension of *state* power over the vulnerable in the past century and the most expensive, complicated and inequitable social policy. It epitomizes a phrase made famous by Hannah Arendt, 'the banality of evil'. Each step in its edifice might be a minor source of inequity. But the total edifice is causing great suffering and humiliation to a growing proportion of the British population. When fully rolled out, one in three British households and nearly half of all the children in Britain will be enmeshed in it.

UC is an instrument of state paternalism, which is ironic since Conservatives boast they are against 'the nanny state' and say they believe in freedom. Under UC, 'welfare claimants' are told they will receive benefits only if they do what their bureaucratic minders tell them, which may be hard for them to do or in some cases even to know what to do.

UC is not simply suffering from 'teething problems', due to its extraordinary complexity, nor can the scheme be fixed just by raising the stingy level of benefits, or by tweaking some of the rules. Its conception and design are fundamentally flawed. In fact, UC is *morally* flawed.

Iain Duncan Smith, the Conservative secretary of state at the Department for Work and Pensions (DWP) responsible for its design, stated that he wanted UC to be as close to being in a job as possible.

To receive benefit, applicants must sign a contract imposing daily obligations and are subject to sanctions if they are not deemed to be looking hard enough for jobs, miss appointments or even if they are a few minutes late. At the same time the DWP is closing job centres, making travel to them for appointments more difficult, expensive and time-consuming.

The scheme's designers initially instituted a six-week wait before UC could be paid, later reduced to five weeks, claiming this would induce claimants to 'learn financial management'. Unlike a job, they are not given back-pay for those weeks. And in practice, many have had to wait much longer. In 2018, the National Audit Office (NAO) reported that in the previous year a quarter of all new entitled claimants were not paid on time, with payment delayed on average by four weeks. About 40% of late-paid claimants had to wait 11 weeks or more. Ensuring that claimants do not have any money to manage is a strange way of enabling them to manage their finances.

In response to the predictable hardship and suffering this has caused, the DWP makes short-term loans to desperate households which then have to be paid back from their meagre benefits as soon as they eventually receive them. This deduction can be up to 40% of benefits (the DWP is considering lowering this to 30%), leaving people in utter penury. Remarkably, given the statistics and the many reports of individuals in distress, the DWP was still claiming in March 2019 that 'on universal credit, no one has to wait five weeks to be paid'. That statement was made in response to widely reported stories of women resorting to prostitution because they were not receiving their UC payments.[2]

The Trussell Trust, which runs more than 400 food banks, reported that they were more than four times as busy in areas where the full UC service had been in place for 12 months or more as elsewhere in the country. Nearly three quarters of people referred to its food banks because they were forced to wait for benefits to be paid fell further into debt.

UC imposes sanctions on claimants deemed not to have complied with imposed obligations. The nanny state says this is to improve their behaviour and 'social integration'. But despite government claims, sanctions or the threat of them do not improve people's motivation to seek, prepare for or take jobs. The opposite appears to be the case.[3] Meanwhile, an NAO report concluded that the DWP spends between £30 million and £50 million a year applying sanctions and about £200 million monitoring the terms it sets for job seekers. In 2015 it 'saved' only £132 million in benefits withheld but the net benefit saving was much lower because it had to make hardship payments amounting to £35 million to sanctioned claimants. So, the savings were equivalent to less than half the cost of monitoring and applying sanctions. The NAO said it could not estimate the extra costs occasioned by sanctions to other parts of the public sector, such as the NHS.[4]

Other defects of UC include the following:

The two-child limit: Since April 2017 benefits are paid only for the first and second child, effectively punishing children in larger families. This has been coupled with the infamous rape clause stating that benefit can be paid for a subsequent child if a woman can *prove* that child was the result of rape. In January 2019, the work and pensions secretary announced that the rule would no longer apply to children born before April 2017 but would apply to those born after that date. Denying benefits to children who are not a first or second child is crude class-based policy. The DWP had the cheek to describe this as 'a key part of controlling public spending'.[5]

Payment by household: By giving the benefit only to one designated household member, UC can entrench the power of abusive men over their woman partner. In January 2019, the DWP announced it was considering giving it to 'the main carer'. That might be better, but it would still fail to treat people as individuals. At the same time, the DWP said pensioners with a partner under pension age would have to apply for UC, rather than having existing benefits transferred. This move, supposedly related to work incentives, will lead to more pensioners losing benefits.

The minimum income floor for the self-employed and in-work conditionality: Built into UC is a sly reduction in entitlements for the precariat – the nominally self-employed, agency workers and zero-hour contract employees who have irregular hours and income. The self-employed may receive hundreds of pounds a year less in benefit than someone in a full-time job on the same annual income. This is because entitlement to UC is subject to a 'minimum income floor'. If a person is self-employed for a year or more, it is presumed that they are earning the equivalent of the (hourly) national minimum wage for at least 35 hours a week. If they earn less than this, UC will not make up the difference. But if they earn more their benefit is reduced. The DWP, which introduced the minimum income floor ostensibly to weed out claims based on bogus or non-viable businesses, says the rule 'encourages' people to find more opportunities to earn money, ignoring the fact that for many those opportunities do not exist, which is why they are claiming benefit in the first place.

Meanwhile, UC claimants with paid jobs must be working a minimum number of hours or show they are trying to do so, under pain of sanctions. The extra hours may simply not be available. And seeking them may clash with the requirements of their existing employer; for example, if they need to be on call, with irregular schedules, that may prevent them from committing to another job.

Lack of due process: Both the six means-tested benefits that UC is replacing ('legacy benefits') and UC itself fail to respect due process. For example, employees sacked for alleged misconduct are automatically subject to a benefits sanction, preventing them from claiming JSA for at least 13 weeks.[6] The DWP simply takes the word of the employer. Individuals only have a right of appeal in limited circumstances.

The sanctions regime also violates due process. Bureaucrats can summarily withhold benefits for deemed failure to fulfil contractual obligations. The number of benefit claimants sanctioned far exceeds the number of people fined in magistrates' and sheriffs' courts for proven crimes and misdemeanours, and they are subject to more severe punishment than those found guilty in those courts, even though decisions on sanctions are made in secret by officials with no statutory responsibility to act lawfully.[7]

The high number of successful appeals shows that many of these decisions are arbitrary and unfair. But in the meantime, claimants must go without the income they need to survive. The stress entailed by the procedure, the difficulty of navigating the rules and fear of being labelled a troublemaker will deter many others from appealing against an unjustified decision.

High administration costs: The NAO reported in 2018 that on average each UC claim costs the DWP £699, against a supposed target cost of £173.[8] There are also extra administrative costs borne by local authorities that the NAO was unable to estimate. During 2018, implicitly admitting that the system was in chaos, if not meltdown, the government turned to Citizens Advice to help with claims and other support.

Under-qualified employees: Employees dealing with applicants are woefully under-qualified to make judgements on benefit claims.

A Citizens Advice worker told me about an Irish claimant denied benefits to which she was entitled because the JobCentrePlus adviser said, 'Southern Ireland isn't in the European Union.' The Citizens Advice expert responded, 'Yes, the Republic of Ireland is in it.' The JCPlus adviser retorted, 'No, it isn't.' 'Er – please check with your manager.' 'I have, and it isn't.' It took over a year for the claimant to obtain her legitimate benefits.

Under-funding: UC has been a way of cutting the level of benefits. The work and pensions secretary finally admitted in October 2018 that many families would be worse off under UC than under the legacy benefits. Half of lone parents and two-thirds of couples with children stand to lose £2,400 a year under the new system. This did not stop the DWP from spending thousands of pounds on cakes for staff to celebrate the roll-out, as witnessed in Belfast.[9]

Online applications: Claimants must apply for benefits online. Yet many of those who need UC do not have easy access to computers or are unfamiliar with using them. They are being directed to computers in public libraries or to advice centres. But under the government's austerity policy, many public libraries have been closed and, especially in rural areas, people may have to make lengthy and costly journeys, perhaps on several occasions, to the nearest library or advice centre.

UC is *workfare*. It requires people to undertake a stressful time-using set of practices every day that intensify feelings of insecurity, anxiety and stigma. This is not incidental or unintended; it is the objective. As one whistle-blower official bitterly recounted, 'We are punishing claimants for not understanding a system that is not built with them in mind.'

The following box summarizes the main flaws in UC:

---

1. Means-testing ➜ low take up, high exclusion errors, poverty trap, precarity trap.

2. High administration costs – due to complexity, intrusive check-ups on claimants, operation of bureaucrats dealing with 'contracts', and so on.

3. Inefficiency – due to complexity and arbitrary nature of tests to which claimants are subjected.

4. Delays in payments ➜ resultant stress, debt, hardship, child poverty ➜ homelessness, use of food banks, ill-health, suicides.

5. Sanctions ➜ stress, debt, hardship, child poverty ➜ homelessness, use of food banks, ill-health, suicides.

6. Lack of due process – due to failure to respect common justice in determining entitlement and in imposing sanctions.

7. Targeting misses the targets – due to the fact that the scheme is deliberately onerous and intrusive.

8. Unfairness in excluding third and any subsequent children from benefits, so lowering benefits for *all* children in larger families.

9. It limits freedom – due to the imposition of constraints on claimants and the bureaucratic directions imposed on them that are not imposed on other groups in society.

Throwing more money at UC will not overcome its moral and structural failings. A high proportion of the money being spent on the system goes on administration, on legal cases around appeals, on lavish contracts given to private firms (Capita and Atos) and so-called charities, and on procedural paperwork, rather than on giving people in need proper economic and social security. It is crying out for wholesale reform, not for further tinkering.

In late 2018, the DWP announced that Citizens Advice, long held in high esteem as a charity representing the citizens against the state, had signed a government contract for £51 million to help in the delivery of UC. They thereby forfeited their right to be regarded as a gatekeeper of common rights. Shortly afterwards it was revealed that other charities had signed contracts to assist the DWP that now include a commitment not to criticize the department or the minister.[10] They had sold themselves and should be denied tax advantages gained by being a registered charity.

That is surely a litany of flaws to justify scrapping UC as soon as possible, beginning with a cessation of sanctions.[11] By contrast, a basic income would be paid automatically as a right. People would not have to fulfil conditions to receive it, and there would be no delays in payment and no due process issues associated with sanctions. And administration costs would be far lower, since there would be no need for a large bureaucracy to monitor claimants and assess individual claims.

Reviving and enhancing disability benefits

Part of the benefit system for those with disability is being folded into UC. There are currently two main benefits for those with disabilities, the Employment Support Allowance (ESA), which is means-tested, and the misnamed Personal Independence Payment (PIP), which is based on tests of a person's 'capacity to work'. The latter replaced the Disability Living Allowance (DLA), which was based on the principle that society owes those with impairments a contribution to their extra costs of living.

The abolition of DLA by the Coalition government in 2013 was explicitly intended to reduce the number of people receiving disability benefits and the amount that many others received. Further restrictions were introduced subsequently. The system is now designed not to meet the needs of those with disabilities but to force as many as possible to do as much as possible to obtain jobs or put in more hours.[12] This reorientation alters the whole ethos of the system.

As a result of their design, both ESA and PIP have high exclusion errors – many people entitled to them do not obtain them – and introduce perverse incentives for applicants to act in ways that are not in their best interest. For example, if a person with severe walking difficulties makes an effort to walk more than the specified 20 metres, they may be denied the higher PIP mobility payment. If someone else with a similar physical condition does not make such painful effort, they do obtain the benefit. The policy obviously penalizes the 'striver'.

People with episodic illnesses such as epilepsy or depression may be declared fit on one day but have terrible affliction on another. People with degenerative illness or terminal cancer have also been found fit to work. An audit by the DWP itself found that one in every three PIP assessment reports completed by the private firm Capita between April and December 2016 contained errors or omitted relevant information, rendering decisions made on them suspect or simply wrong.[13] The Work Capability Assessment test itself has been acknowledged by one of its own designers to be 'imperfect', and has been subject to a withering critique as 'bogus' and largely driven by the commercial concerns of Unum, a US-based insurance corporation that promotes it.[14]

Commercial interests certainly do intrude. Capita and Maximus, the other company involved in making the assessments for PIP, are paid handsomely for doing so. Maximus has been charging the DWP £240 for each assessment, after which the DWP must decide whether to accept the result, costing the public even more. And administrative costs do not stop there. By 2018, the DWP and Ministry of Justice were spending over £200 million annually to deal with 'mandatory reconsiderations' and appeals against ESA and PIP decisions. It is a scathing indictment that an astonishing two-thirds of all PIP and ESA claimants had the decision to deny them benefits overturned at 'mandatory reconsideration' stage or later won their appeals at the tribunal.[15] But meanwhile they had to endure the stress and hardship of an unreliable and protracted process.

The PIP scheme has been particularly severe on people with episodic disabilities. Some 54% of those who had been receiving DLA in 2013 were rejected for its PIP replacement, and it scarcely justifies the scheme that 78% of those who appealed eventually obtained their benefits, after many months of anxiety and probable ill-health.

The complexity of the system makes it prone to error. An egregious example came to light in 2018 when Parliament's Public Accounts Committee (PAC) found that the DWP, having discovered in 2014 that some 70,000 disabled people had been denied benefits unfairly since 2011, had concealed the knowledge and continued to underpay them for another three years until the PAC exposed the error.

Shockingly, the DWP said it would only make back payments to 2014 when it discovered the error. Even so, the department was liable for over £340 million in back payments and £14 million in extra administration costs. Yet nobody resigned or was 'sanctioned'. A system that penalizes claimants late for an interview by withdrawing vital benefits, while major life-changing errors and dishonesty go unpunished, is plainly immoral.

The cost in human life is rather greater. In late 2018, the DWP was forced to admit that every day about 100 people were dying while on one or other of the disability benefits and that about 10 people died every day who had been deemed by the DWP as 'fit for work'.[16]

The current disability benefit system is unfit for purpose and lacks a moral compass. Benefits for those with impairments should be based on medical criteria determined by independent medical experts, not by employees of commercial firms paid to operate benefit policies with incentives to reduce 'costs'. As Disabled People Against Cuts rightly argues, the present system has 'too many flaws to be simply paused and fixed' and is 'rotten to the core'. An ideal system would move away from the notion of perceived need to one of providing everybody with equal good opportunity to develop their potential and enjoy a good life.[17]

If a basic income system were introduced, those with disabilities would be entitled to *separate* additional benefits based on actuarial estimates of the extra costs of living and the lower earnings people with specific impairments could expect. Using more objective criteria would help to defuse suspicion of 'faking', which has led to incidents of abuse of disabled people, and would institutionalize an essential ethic of basic income – compassion (not pity).

3

Why basic income beats the alternatives

Besides the ethical justification for basic income outlined earlier and its potential for combating the eight modern giants, there are several other arguments for moving towards a basic income as an anchor for a new distribution system.

It is impossible to consider social policy reform in 2019 without reference to Brexit. Although at the time of writing, the outcome was still unclear, Brexit in whatever form will involve considerable 'collateral damage', in lives thrown into disarray and worse. Having a basic income in place, even one that paid a fraction of what is required for a decent living standard, would help ameliorate the disruptive costs of Brexit, which will surely be borne by many of those least able to bear them.

A basic income would complement a much-needed radical new housing policy, including reversing the decline in social housing and imposing rent controls. For the time being, however, Housing Benefit would need to be retained.

A basic income would reward unpaid work, so would encourage people to spend more time doing care work. As an ageing society, Britain is suffering a substantial and growing 'care deficit'. A basic income would enable more people to care for those they love, thereby reducing pressure on public spending for care services. In considering the net cost of a basic income, this expected saving should be factored into the calculations.

A basic income could also act as a suitable macro-economic stabilizer, with a core payment, adjusted according to changes in real per capita income, and a cyclical component, which would rise in times of recession and fall in times of 'full employment' or high aggregate demand.[1] A basic income system would also tend to lessen regional inequality: it would represent a higher share of per capita income in low-income areas and encourage desirable inter-regional mobility.

Sensible, modern business folk, including leading entrepreneurs and CEOs of mainstream corporations, also understand that basically secure people make more cooperative and productive workers, and even more rational consumers. Those on the political left should not be cynical about the fact that leading entrepreneurs such as Elon Musk and Richard Branson have come out in favour of basic income.

There is growing evidence that a basic income has popular support and the potential for much more, contrary to jaundiced views by prominent figures who have not studied the subject.[2] Two types of evidence are worth mentioning. Some years ago, a team of social psychologists conducted experiments in deliberative democracy covering large samples in three countries, in which people were asked to decide which of four options of fair distribution policy should have precedence. They had to choose from behind a 'veil of ignorance', that is, not knowing where they themselves would be in the distribution system.[3] In initial votes, the majority in all cases chose the income floor, or basic income, option. But the most instructive outcome was that when the groups were requested to discuss the issues and vote again, many more voted for the income floor option. Deliberative debate may help engender stronger public support.[4]

More topical evidence comes from recent opinion polls in the UK. A European-wide survey that included the UK found strong public support.[5] But one survey, commissioned by the Royal Society of Arts and known as the Populus survey, has gone further by focusing on the reasons for views for or against. Overall, 41% of respondents were in favour, and 17% against, with the remainder saying they did not know or were neutral. Because more women were unsure, more men were in favour and fewer women were against. Nevertheless, the results implied that more than twice as many were in favour as against. Unsurprisingly, support dropped when people were asked if they would support it if income tax was used to pay for it. Attitudes to other financing options were not explored.

By contrast, only 19% of respondents said that the current system was adequate and that there was no need to experiment with a basic income. Some 45% said they thought it would do a better job of ensuring security than the current system. More than 56% said they thought it would encourage more work by removing the current disincentives. And 49% agreed with the statement that it would reduce the stigma associated with receiving benefits. Taking account of the 'don't knows', in each case there was a substantial majority in favour.

A final justification for basic income is not quantifiable but is potentially important for rebuilding social solidarity and society. Basic income paid to all usual residents would help to restore faith in an enabling (or 'empowering') state, combating the state paternalism and the growth of the panopticon state that have been powerful trends in the first two decades of this century.

Answering the objections

(1) A basic income would not work.

Much of the controversy surrounding basic income has been due to misunderstanding and misrepresentation. The idea is simply that everybody should be provided with basic economic security. This has not stopped critics from claiming that advocates want to dismantle the welfare state and that it would be totally unaffordable. Their claims should remind us of standard reactions to every new transformative policy, elegantly summarized by the late great political economist Albert Hirschmann, on grounds of futility (it would not work), perversity (it would have unintended negative consequences) and jeopardy (it would endanger other goals).[6]

Hirschmann pointed out that the standard reactions were voiced against unemployment benefits and family benefits and other benefits that we now take for granted, and went on to show that once introduced such objections tend to melt away, to be replaced by claims that the policy was 'common sense' and even inevitable. Family allowances are a classic example. In the 1920s, the idea was seen as an issue for cranks and utopians. By 1946, every British family with more than one child was receiving a family allowance.

(2) A basic income is unaffordable.

Some politicians and commentators have asserted that a basic income would be unaffordable without a big rise in direct taxes. These calculations assume that basic income from the outset would replace all existing benefits. However, like pension reform and other changes to the social protection system, basic income could be introduced gradually. There would still be savings from a reduction in means-tested benefit payments.[7] And there are other ways of paying for a basic income without sharp increases in income tax, including from a Commons Fund.

That said, there is scope for tax increases. The tax take in Britain is 35% of GDP, which is low by past standards and by comparison with other comparable countries. It averages 40% in the EU and 47% in France. Britain also spends a much lower share of national income on benefits than most European countries.

Rolling back the extraordinary number of existing tax reliefs, over 1,150 at the last count, would also free up funds for a new distribution system without raising income tax rates. Tax reliefs are distortionary and mostly regressive, benefiting the rich far more than low earners and of no benefit whatever to half the adult population with incomes below the tax threshold. For the 209 'principal reliefs', costing the Treasury £50 million or more, foregone revenue was estimated at over £430 billion in 2018–19. Not all of that could be easily obtained, but modification to the tax system would clearly make a basic income affordable.

For instance, abolition of the personal allowance before income tax kicks in, increased to £12,500 in 2019–20, would raise over £111 billion a year. The allowance is worth more than £6,500 to the 10% richest families and only £600 on average to the poorest 10%. As Andrew Harrop, director of the Fabian Society, memorably described the current personal allowance policy, it is 'regressive universalism'.[8]

A report by the New Economics Foundation (NEF) in March 2019 recommended scrapping the allowance and replacing it by a payment of £48 a week to every adult over the age of 18, barring the richest 1%, and an increase in Child Benefit.[9] Although the NEF's head of economics claimed this would not be a step towards a basic income, it is hard to see why it could not be.[10] Such a 'partial' basic income, as proposed by Labour MP Karen Buck and her colleague Declan Gaffney,[11] would not only be more progressive than the tax allowance, redistributing from rich to poor. People would also know in advance how much would be coming in each week or month and could plan on that basis, another valuable advantage of basic income.

The Fabian Society has also proposed converting the personal tax allowance and Child Benefit into a system of 'universal individual credits'. They would have two features of a basic income – they would be paid in cash and to individuals, not families or households.[12] But the proposal envisages continuation of the means-tested Universal Credit (UC) and is also conditional: 'Eligibility for the adult credits should depend on paying direct taxes or on productive participation in society.' It would thus be a back route into workfare, which no progressive government should promote.

Tax relief on pension contributions, which benefits those fortunate enough to have employers contributing to workplace pensions, and especially higher-rate taxpayers, costs the Exchequer about £26 billion.[13] Slashing the capital gains tax exemption for selling a property designated as a main home, another regressive tax relief, would free up £27 billion. And over a billion could be liberated by abolishing the Personal Savings Allowance and the Dividend Allowance, both tax privileges for the relatively rich with substantial incomes from savings and investments. Those five measures alone would yield more than enough to pay a basic income of £48 a week without cutting any other benefits.

Other regressive tax reliefs that could be scrapped include the Business Property Relief from inheritance tax that is supposed to benefit small businesses but actually benefits some of the wealthiest families in the UK, denying the Exchequer some £700 million a year. Inheritance tax loopholes overall cost about £2 billion a year. Additional finance could be raised by tackling the widespread tax avoidance by wealthy individuals and corporations, which has been allowed and even facilitated to a much greater extent in the UK than in other countries.[14]

There are other ways of showing how a basic income could be afforded. Some commentators propose funding basic income through monetary policy, a form of 'quantitative easing for people' instead of the Bank of England's 'quantitative easing' policy of releasing money to the financial markets. This could be a means of redressing a structural failing of the British economy, the increasing lag of aggregate wage income behind GDP growth, which is resulting in rising debt as households try to maintain living standards by borrowing to pay for goods and services.[15]

Stewart Lansley and Howard Reed, in a report for Compass, have proposed a three-step approach for phasing in a full basic income. Their first step would be to convert the existing personal tax allowance into a payment to everybody of £25 a week in the first year (which with the raising of the allowance would now be higher). This would be followed by a series of up-ratings over the next nine years that would subsequently be paid from the annual returns generated by creation of a citizens' wealth fund.[16]

In a similar vein, the Royal Society of Arts has proposed a 'universal basic opportunity fund' financed from long-term bonds that could pay out an 'opportunity dividend' in a lump-sum payment.[17] This offers a capital grant rather than a basic income, but is seen by the authors as a step towards it. Capital grants nevertheless have significant drawbacks: most notably, they do not provide basic security, since once they are spent, wisely or not, there is no guaranteed regular income in prospect. The same concern arises from the interesting proposal from the Institute for Public Policy Research for a national fund that would provide every 25-year-old with a capital dividend of £10,000 from the year 2030.[18]

As I argue elsewhere, the optimal way to finance a rising basic income would be to create a more general Commons Fund, which would pay out common dividends that would rise gradually as the fund grew.[19] It would be built mainly from levies on commercial intrusions into the commons, boosted by contributions from a land-value tax, eco taxes, digital information levies and several others. But whatever the financing mechanism, there are ample reasons to be confident that a basic income is affordable.

Moreover, a basic income or common dividend would have economic benefits that would lower the net 'cost', including reduced demand on health services, entry into the tax-paying economy of 'black economy' activity (due to the weakening of poverty and precarity traps), and savings on care costs. It is hard to estimate how great these savings would be, but the evidence (e.g. from the Mincome experiment in Manitoba) suggests they would be significant.

(3)   A basic income would reduce work and encourage laziness.

Ironically, it is the current means-tested benefit system that acts as a systemic disincentive to take low-wage jobs, simply because of the poverty trap and precarity trap discussed earlier. Going from meagre benefits into a low-wage job can result in a marginal tax rate of 80%. So, the person would only gain a little extra, which could become nothing after commuting costs and other work-related expenses are taken into account. The poverty trap is reduced slightly under UC, but still exists. And the precarity trap is greatly worsened. This has led the government to tighten conditions, a sure sign that it recognizes there is no incentive to take jobs for those at the lower-income end of the labour market.

Even the World Bank, in its 2018 *World Development Report*, admitted that the evidence showed that basic income did not reduce work.[20] A study of one prominent scheme, the Alaska Permanent Fund and Dividends, found that it resulted in a big increase in part-time employment and an increase in employment overall.[21] There is extensive evidence that basic income promotes more work and more productive labour.

Most recently, the basic income experiment in Finland (see Appendix A) found that removing the condition that the unemployed had to search for jobs made no difference to employment, and the basic income pilot in Ontario found that it induced a substantial increase in voluntary work.

(4) A basic income would be 'something-for-nothing'.

In fact, it would represent a modest social 'dividend' on our common wealth, a form of public inheritance. The criticism is particularly hypocritical coming from those who manage to have no objection to vast inherited wealth or to the numerous regressive subsidies for which recipients have done nothing, including the hundreds of selective tax reliefs for special interests. More positively, as a basic income could be expected to give ordinary people more security and confidence and thus empower them, it could generate 'something for something' – more work and more productive labour.

(5) Why give money to the rich?

A quasi-universal system would strengthen feelings of social solidarity. But, more pragmatically, distributing to everybody would be more efficient, less expensive and more equitable – without risking the high exclusion errors that always arise with targeted policies that are only for 'the poor'. There is also the counterargument that means-testing everybody to determine entitlement to the basic income would be ridiculously complicated and costly.

Since the basic income would not be withdrawn as earnings rose, it would begin to eliminate the poverty trap and the precarity trap. And it could be clawed back from above-median income earners through the tax system, leaving their net income unchanged.

(6)   A basic income would be a threat to the welfare state.

Some supporters of basic income on the libertarian right have seen it as a means of dismantling the welfare state. But this is not the position of most basic income advocates, who support the strengthening, not weakening, of public services. Right-wing libertarians want to dismantle the state in general. But their posture should be combated in general. As it is, the welfare state has been made more fragile and 'residual' in character as successive governments have accelerated the trends to comprehensive means-testing, behavioural conditionality and workfare. None of the funding methods envisaged for basic income would mean less money for public services.

(7)   Basic income would weaken unions and collective bargaining.

Some trade unionists have argued that, if workers had a basic income, they would not join unions and would be less inclined to push for higher wages. The opposite is the case. It would encourage workers to back collective bargaining for higher wages, because having basic income security would make them less fearful of retribution. A basic income would be a boon to unionism.

(8)   A basic income would subsidize low wages.

Although a basic income could encourage some employers to offer lower wages, it would also strengthen the worker's bargaining position. It would not rise or fall if wages changed, whereas means-tested subsidies (in the form of tax credits and UC) fall as wages rise, reducing the benefit of higher wages and lowering the incentive to push for them. Tax credits exert downward pressure on wages at the lower end of the labour market, particularly for low-wage women. In practice, by depressing wages, about a third of the money spent on them raises the income of employers.[22]

Tax credits are the modern equivalent of the infamous Speenhamland system introduced in England in the late eighteenth century, which accelerated rural pauperization. Besides holding down wages, modern tax credits have almost certainly been a factor depressing productivity growth, seen by many economists as the bane of the British economy. If employers can pay low wages because they will be topped up by tax credits, they will be under less cost pressure to invest and improve management to raise productivity. It is shocking that, in the two decades in which they have been operating, costing as much as £32 billion a year at the maximum, tax credits have never been subject to a formal evaluation. In sum, a basic income would not depress wages, whereas existing tax credits do.

(9) The National Minimum Wage will take care of 'working poverty'.

The statutory National Minimum Wage (dubbed the National Living Wage for workers aged 25 and over) is a moral standard setter. But not too much should be expected from the minimum wage in the flexible labour market of the twenty-first century. It has limited reach to the precariat: for instance, employers can offset minimum wage increases by cutting hours worked or reducing other benefits. However, it would complement a basic income.

Enforcement has been a problem. Every year since the minimum wage was introduced in Britain, hundreds of thousands of workers entitled to it have been paid less, and that has persisted for two decades, even though for much of that time there was a government strongly supporting it.

In 2018, the Low Pay Commission estimated that 580,000 workers were underpaid. If unpaid overtime was included, that rose to two million, or almost a tenth of all employees aged 25 and over. That is probably an underestimate: in a flexible and insecure labour market it is hard to measure what is being paid, while vulnerable workers will be reluctant to report underpayment for fear of retribution from current or future employers. And even when underpayment is established, employers face only mild punishment. Though the maximum fine was 200% of every penny underpaid, while HMRC estimated that rogue employers underpaid staff by £15.6 million in 2017–18, government fines came to only £14 million.

Although the system should be made more efficient, it is unlikely that a minimum wage could ever be close to watertight. But people with a basic income would be more confident and less fearful in reporting abuse.

(10)   People do not support basic income.

This was encouragingly refuted by the Populus poll mentioned earlier and by other opinion poll results. But there is still a need for more informed public debate. Where and when that happens, popular support grows considerably. In the Populus poll, the biggest objections to basic income among those who opposed it were the belief that it was unaffordable (73%) and that it would disincentivize work (72%).

There was a strong correlation between support for basic income and views on affordability and work, suggesting these are (as expected) issues on which to put emphasis and convince the electorate that basic income is affordable and will not reduce the propensity to work. Those undecided on basic income were also the most likely to be unsure about affordability and work, again suggesting that if properly informed they could be enlisted to support it.

Those who saw the role of the welfare state as 'supporting the vulnerable' were most likely to favour basic income, by 3:1. Those who saw the role of the welfare state as supporting 'traditional values' were the least likely to support it, although more still supported it than opposed it (39% to 31%). This group was also the most likely to think that basic income could reduce crime (52% to 17%) and that it would increase personal agency (62%). These perspectives are intriguing in suggesting lines of public debate. But none of the results suggest that the public is hostile to basic income. The reverse would seem to be the case.

4

Piloting basic income in Britain

As stated at the outset, the case for a basic income is fundamentally ethical, strengthened by its transformative potential in building a new income distribution system. If that case were accepted, there would be no necessity for pilots before introducing basic income as policy. However, if properly designed and implemented, pilots could help in the policy legitimation process. They could deal with the most obvious claims for or against it, such as the effects on work and labour, on mental and physical health, and social attitudes. They could also indicate the likely resultant savings in other public spending.

Past pilots (summarized in Appendix A), particularly in North America, have given most attention to labour supply issues, followed by the impact on health and schooling, both of which have been positive. Of course, these issues should be given attention in any pilots carried out in the UK. However, it would be desirable to give more attention to the possible impact on the modern 'giants' outlined earlier, notably stress, insecurity, debt and unpaid work including care work and volunteering.

One potentially valuable feature of pilots would be the demonstration of positive feedback effects. For instance, there is already other evidence that basic income security leads to less stress and mental illness. If pilots confirmed this effect, it would imply that the net cost of a basic income would be much less than the gross cost. Fewer demands would be made on the NHS and fewer workdays would be lost to absenteeism or low-productivity 'presenteeism'. Testing for such possibilities should be built into the design of any pilot and the evaluation instruments.

Several countries have found that just the existence of pilots, or even plans for them, can stimulate more dispassionate and informed discussion about basic income. They can thus help to overcome prejudices, such as the most common of all, that basic income will make people 'lazy'.

Pilots could also be useful as a means of exploring how a basic income should or could be phased into reality. They would be a form of demonstration project.[1] They could also test what, if any, other policies or institutional changes would be desirable to make the introduction of basic income more successful. A variant of this approach would have two similar communities, in one of which basic incomes would be paid but where no other action was taken, and in the other – in addition to the basic income – an independent non-governmental body would be charged in some way with giving advice and assistance to recipients.

For instance, in pilots in India a basic income was paid to everybody in four communities where there were no collective bodies to represent workers and disadvantaged groups in their dealings with others, and also in four similar communities where SEWA (the Self-Employed Women's Association) was operational and available to advise and assist people in making decisions.[2] A similar design could be considered in the UK and even incorporate funding to compensate a collective body, perhaps a union, for providing such guidance.

Attitudes matter. One widely held view, encapsulated in the eighth 'giant' and supported by considerable evidence, is that people's income security affects their sense of altruism, their tolerance of strangers and ultimately their attitudes to democratic values and authoritarianism. Several pilots have strongly suggested that basic income has a positive impact on all those elements, and thus could be healthy for society, something that is rarely taken into account by critics. People's opinions at the outset and at the end of the pilots could be compared, and compared with those of a control group not receiving the basic income.

Pilots in the UK could help policymakers factor these issues into their decisions. It should also be borne in mind that community effects may be greater than if only a few individuals are provided with such security, so encouraging pilots that give a basic income to all in a community rather than to randomly chosen individuals.

One obstacle in the way of pilots is greater in the UK than in somewhere like India. The existing tax and benefit systems are so complex and well entrenched that it would be hard to displace them for the purpose of testing a different system. As the preparation of pilots in Scotland and also in California has found, this is a significant problem when the government is not supportive. The same applies to the need to gain administrative approval and cooperation.

From a political point of view, perhaps the biggest danger is that pilots become an excuse to postpone actual policy development and implementation. While pilots are in progress, feasibility plans and the funding base could be established in the expectation that the pilots would show what besides the actual payments would make the policy optimally successful. And it should be borne in mind that ultimately the justification for basic income or common dividends is social justice.

What should be piloted?

Recalling the characteristics described at the outset, basic income is quasi-universal (not means-tested), unconditional, individual and non-withdrawable. A pilot should test each of those characteristics, by comparison with the existing system. But a specific pilot need not necessarily test *all* the elements to be useful.

The primary rule in designing pilots is that they should respect the characteristics of basic income. This does not mean that any one pilot should exactly mirror what a basic income system would be, because we might want to test the feasibility and impact of some aspects without dealing with others. The ideal would replicate what a basic income would be in every respect. But for practical reasons, trying to operationalize the ideal might be the enemy of piloting something sufficiently good to help justify the ideal.

Thus, we might want to test whether behavioural conditionality is necessary or equitable or efficient, while maintaining a means-test of some sort. Or we might want to test whether different amounts paid would alter the impact on behaviour, perhaps in affecting the propensity to reduce or increase work and labour. However, as far as possible, as many characteristics of an ideal basic income as possible should apply – a basic amount, paid to all usual residents, paid regularly, without behavioural conditions and non-withdrawable.

The following should be absolute rules:

(A) The basic income must be paid to each individual. Each man and each woman should receive an equal basic income, paid directly to them and not to a 'household head', unless there is a mental health condition making it advisable to pay to the principal 'carer'. Paying individually is a vital feminist principle, which has been systematically abused in all social security systems over the past century, including Universal Credit.

(B)   The basic income must be unconditional, in three senses – past activities, present status and use of the basic income. Recipients should not be required to spend the money in any specific way.

(C)   The basic income must be non-withdrawable. It should be clear and guaranteed to recipients that they will not have their basic income withdrawn during the course of the pilot for any reason other than a permanent move out of the area.

For the purpose of a pilot, the amount paid as a basic income need not be judged by short-term affordability at national level. The pilot could be realistically aspirational, setting amounts that the government could aim to afford within the lifetime of a five-year electoral term, but which might be deemed impractical for cost reasons in the first year of government. While the funding mechanisms for a national scheme, such as a permanent capital fund, are being assembled, pilots that would be hard to afford without them could be tested and evaluated.

With those points in mind, this book recommends five types of basic income pilot:

- *Model A: Basic income instead of means-tested benefits.* A sample of people – a whole community defined as a locality – would be provided with basic incomes, with additional separate benefits for those with special needs. The basic income would be provided instead of existing means-tested benefits, with the exception of Housing Benefit, which should be retained (or be replaced by an equivalent to compensate for any loss of the housing element of UC). Provisionally, it is proposed that every adult in a selected community would be provided with £100 a week, with £50 for each child and with additional separate benefits for those with disabilities. As indicated later, the selection of the community should be random and be drawn from a group of low-income communities.[3]

This model should be regarded as realistically aspirational, recognizing that funding such a scheme nationally would involve a significant cost that would have to be met by tax increases, diversion of public spending from other uses (such as subsidies and tax reliefs) or the establishment of a Commons Fund as described earlier. A primary purpose of this model would be to determine whether the benefits of such a scheme – such as improved health, reduced stress, more work and less crime, as found in pilots elsewhere – would merit consideration of this option in the future.

- *Model B: Basic income alongside existing benefits.* A sample of people – again, preferably all members of an identifiable locality – would be provided with basic incomes of £70 per week for working-age adults, and £20 per week for children on top of Child Benefit. Tax codes for every recipient would be changed to impose the basic rate of income tax on all earned income below the higher-rate tax threshold. Means-tested benefits would be left in place, but basic incomes would be added to the means taken into account. Each recipient household's means-tested benefits would thus be automatically adjusted downwards by the basic income and upwards by the change in net earnings brought about by the tax code change. Administration of the scheme would be possible if the recipient community were to be defined by postcode boundaries and the government was able to instruct HMRC and DWP to make the necessary changes within the recipient community.[4]

- *Model C: Basic income added to existing benefits.* A sample of people – again, preferably everybody in a local community – would be provided with a basic income as a supplement to their existing state benefits. This would be firmly in the spirit of common dividends, and the per capita amount could be less than in the first two models. One option might be to provide every adult in a community with a tax-free £50 per week for one year that was not taken into account in determining access to means-tested benefits. This would strengthen income security and be progressive, since the amount would represent a larger proportion of the income of a low-income person than for others.

- *Model D: Scrapping conditions for means-tested benefits.* A sample of adult welfare recipients would have conditions for entitlement to existing means-tested benefits removed, so as to make the benefits closer to a basic income, notably by removing forms of behavioural conditionality that permeate UC and other benefits at the moment. This type of experiment is close to the Finnish scheme and what is currently being tested in the Netherlands (Appendix A). It would have minimal net cost and might even save public money.

- *Model E: Cash for the homeless.* A fifth type of experiment is very different from the others. Sadly relevant to the austerity era, which has seen a horrifying growth of homelessness across the country, it would be a refinement of an approach taken in the City of London some years ago. As described in Appendix A, a small group of long-term rough sleepers were given cash to spend on what they felt was needed to help them off the streets. This led to the majority obtaining places to stay and reconnecting with family and society. This experiment should be repeated in a few other, randomly chosen places. It should not be made a national policy, but the results could be taken into account in formulating and implementing a national basic income system.

At least one of each of the five types of pilot should be undertaken.[5] Indeed, depending on available funds, more than one of Models A, B or C should be conducted, along with four of Model E. The last would be the least expensive, the most easily introduced and the most urgent. For each of the other four models (A, B, C, D) a fund of up to £5 million should be budgeted. That would not be just for 'research', since in each case the community would benefit from the increase in income security that the changes would bring. The exact budget for any pilot would depend on the size of community, its earnings profile and duration of the pilot.

Three other variants might be considered. The first, a 'participation income', was proposed by the late economist Sir Tony Atkinson, who thought basic income would be easier to introduce if it were made conditional on performing a certain amount of work – he proposed 35 hours a week – which might be care work or voluntary work, and not necessarily in paid jobs. [6]

If this were simply a *moral* commitment, rather than one incurring sanctions if not followed, there should be no objection. But it raises several practical problems, including the difficulty of identifying and measuring non-wage work, especially counting hours spent on care. Another objection is that Atkinson's proposed participation conditions would exclude only 1% of the population from receiving the participation income, at a huge cost of intrusive bureaucratic enquiry into every individual's daily activities.[7] And the participation condition might lead back to workfare and a drive to push people into low-paying jobs.[8]

A different proposal has been made by this writer. On first registering to receive the basic income or common dividends, everybody should be required to make a moral commitment (not legally binding) to vote in general elections and to participate in local political meetings at least once a year. This might be called the Pericles Condition, since it roughly corresponds to what happened in ancient Greek democracy. It would be a useful condition to be added to at least one variant of the above models and would be relevant for assessing the drift to populism, the eighth giant threatening a Good Society. The primary hypothesis would be that increased economic security would induce more altruistic political attitudes.

A final variant that could be piloted is a capital grant scheme, where all recipients would be given a one-off grant at the outset, similar to winning a lottery prize or coming into a big inheritance. As mentioned earlier, the Institute for Public Policy Research (IPPR) has proposed a £10,000 'universal minimum inheritance'. And a report by the Friends Provident Foundation floated the idea of an unconditional capital grant of £5,000 to everybody reaching age 25, citing Tom Paine as the inspiration.

However, capital grants have the serious drawback known as 'weakness-of-will'. What happens if recipients 'blow it', which may be the result of excessive risk-taking or just bad luck? Would the state then say, 'Tough; you had your chance'? Or would it have to put the person on some other benefits? The latter course could encourage reckless risk-taking in the first place. Capital grants would also be slightly regressive and would not appeal to all those currently over the age of 25, making it unlikely to pass muster with the majority of voters.

David Willetts, a Conservative politician and president of the Resolution Foundation, has proposed giving £10,000 to every person reaching the age of 30, claiming that this would boost property ownership among the younger population and citing approvingly the sale of council housing in the 1980s.[9] But council house sales cut the supply of affordable housing for those on lower incomes and boosted property prices, increasing wealth inequality. Something similar could be predicted from lump-sum payments, since relatively high-income earners would have access to other funds, while those with only the £10,000 would not. The government's help-to-buy loan scheme is an object lesson. According to a report by the National Audit Office, about three-fifths of buyers could have bought a home without the support, which also pumped up the profits of Britain's biggest housebuilders.[10]

Experience with capital grants elsewhere has shown contradictory effects. They have figured in several of the tribal casino schemes in the United States (Appendix A), where they may have had a spike effect on mortality shortly after receipt, even though for the majority they have had longer-term positive effects on health and education, while lowering crime. In Alaska, recent research showed a small rise in alcohol-related crime immediately after receipt of the annual dividend payment, but the dividends were associated with a reduction in property crime.

Modest regular basic income payments would be better at providing basic security. A poll in the United States found that a majority preferred a regular guaranteed modest basic income to a much larger lump sum, and 46% said they would never switch to a lump sum.[11] That is likely to be the case in the UK as well. For all these reasons, it would not be desirable to conduct a pilot with capital grants.

How should basic income pilots be designed?

Whatever the model to be tested, there are certain design principles that should be followed.[12] First, any pilot or demonstration project should be replicable and upscalable. This rule is not too difficult to respect in the case of basic income experiments. For instance, a local pilot based on Model D – providing existing benefits without behavioural conditions or sanctions – might show that neither conditions nor sanctions are necessary. A critic might claim that this depended on the type of community covered, in which case the pilot could be repeated elsewhere.

It is also highly desirable for basic income pilots to cover a whole community rather than a random (or non-random) sample of individuals or households. Not applying this rule would not invalidate the results in relation to some hypotheses, but would tend to reduce the overall effects, because there are expected community and multiplier effects going beyond those applicable to individuals or their immediate families. Taking even a small community would be preferable to a bigger sample of individuals randomly selected from a large area.

In a test of Model E, in principle all rough sleepers in a definable community should be selected to receive cash help, though without prior warning to avoid attracting incomers. For example, in Hastings, the main homeless charity stated in 2018, 'We've seen a sharp increase in street homelessness and in the first three months of this year we verified 120 different individuals. On any given day we're seeing 49 people rough sleeping now. Last year it was more like 40.'[13] All 49 could be included in a pilot of Model E.

The pilot community should be matched by a control group, that is, an otherwise similar group of people whose situation remains unchanged. Both groups will be subject to the same outside influences, so differences in outcomes can be attributed to the piloted change.[14]

Critics of pilots point out one obvious limitation: they are rarely 'permanent', almost by definition. However, much can be tested and learnt from short-duration pilots. For some behavioural and attitudinal outcomes, there are what might be called 'impact' effects, which occur almost straight away. These may grow or fade away during the course of the pilot. And there are 'learning' effects, as recipients come to realize what the basic income enables them to do or as their security and confidence grow.

For these reasons, pilots should be operational for at least one year and optimally for two years. They should not be much longer, one reason being that they should not be an excuse for delaying a national policy. Lessons can be learnt from as short a period as six months (see Appendix A).

The overall design of a pilot is ultimately a political decision, in that it is necessary to specify what type of payment should be provided, what rules of entitlement should be used, what amounts should be paid and for how long the pilot should last. But the actual implementation and evaluation should be done independently, ideally by university-based teams of qualified researchers.

Fortunately, there is now plenty of experience within the international community of social scientists concerned with basic income, so the process of survey and questionnaire design should be much shorter than it was a few years ago. Policymakers could expect a pilot to be ready to start within a few months of a decision being made. It may be necessary for the political decision makers to indicate which areas of interest should be given high priority. One of the understated lessons from ongoing experiments in the United States is that too many academics have become involved, each with specific and highly sophisticated hypotheses that they would like to see tested with ever-increasing precision. The best can be the enemy of the good.

As for instruments for evaluating pilots, there is no perfect methodology or empirical approach. A mix of methods is good enough. However, there should be detailed quantitative surveys conducted by well-trained and qualified researchers: a baseline survey, that is, a census of all intended recipients and all members of the control group, conducted just before the pilot is launched; and at least two evaluation surveys, one in the middle of the pilot's intended duration, one just before the end of it.[15]

Besides the quantitative study, a more anthropological approach is useful, with detailed case studies to gain impressions from recipients. One advantage is that this can provide valuable information for policymakers more quickly than quantitative survey work. There should also be interviews and information-gathering on community issues from 'key informants', such as local schoolteachers, GPs, local councillors, police, religious leaders from all faiths in the area and trade union representatives.

Should civil society organizations be involved in the project design and implementation? They could not be stopped from being involved in an informal way, if they chose to intervene during the course of a pilot. But some would argue that their formal involvement would bias the results. This would surely not be a negative as long as the intervention was replicable and upscalable to national level as a policy parameter and as long as the organization or organizations were fully independent.

Accordingly, as suggested earlier, at least one pilot (ideally more) could be designed so that in one community a straightforward basic income would be paid to all residents, while in another otherwise similar community an independent Voice organization – perhaps a broadly based trade union or some other representative body – would be made responsible for advice on how recipients might respond to having a basic income. This is under consideration in preparatory work for a pilot in Fife and was successful in pilots in India (see Appendix A). Consideration should also be given to providing such a body with financial assistance to enable it to perform the function more effectively.

Where should pilots be conducted?

Every community in the country should be encouraged to consider applying to be a site for a pilot.

Liverpool has already put itself forward, and some other localities are developing plans, such as Sheffield, where the city council in June 2019 voted to do a pilot, drawing on proposals by a local group, UNILAB.[16] And in Scotland, since 2017 cross-party plans for basic income pilots have been under preparation in four areas – Fife, North Ayrshire, Edinburgh and Glasgow City. Their remit has been to design a scheme that would tackle inequality and provide economic security.

The preparatory work in Scotland has been facilitated by a decision by the Scottish government to make £250,000 available for that work in 2018–20. A steering group involving representatives from all four local councils, the Scottish government and NHS Scotland has been established. A cross-party group has been set up in the Scottish parliament, co-chaired by an Scottish National Party MSP and a Labour MSP, which has been meeting to discuss options since June 2018.[17] The four local authorities will each submit a final business case to Scottish ministers by March 2020.[18] It is to be hoped that these four local initiatives remain cross-party initiatives, since there is certainly interest from across the political spectrum.[19]

In the UK more generally, as in most countries, special dispensation would be required if the basic income were to replace existing means-tested benefits, such as Working Tax Credits, Child Tax Credits and UC (but not Housing Benefit), or if the basic income would be paid in addition to existing benefits, leaving it to the DWP and HMRC to recalculate benefit eligibility and amounts to be paid. HMRC would also need to be involved if different tax codes were to be applied in the pilot communities.

Solely for the purpose of the pilot, one moral condition – or request, since no loss of basic income would follow if it were not respected – should be introduced, which is that all recipients should make a commitment not to do media interviews during the course of the pilot. This would be primarily to protect recipients from unwanted pressure from people who might want to demand some of the money for themselves or interfere to alter their opinions or actions.

Respondents, including all recipients of the basic income, should be assured that any data gathered for evaluation would be used strictly for analytical purposes and would be non-identifiable at a personal level. In several of the negative income tax pilots in the United States, there was some under-reporting of income and employment due to fear that information would be passed to the tax authorities. To compensate for their time in responding to an oral questionnaire, consideration should also be given to providing a modest payment to all those participating in the pilot, whether as recipients or as part of the control group, with payment being made at the end of the pilot.

5

Taking the first steps

A journey of a thousand miles begins with a single step.
LAO TZU, *c.550 BC*

In this book, it has been implicit that whatever is paid as a basic income or common dividend should be paid equally to all deemed eligible. There are arguments for paying different groups different amounts. But in the proposed pilots it seems sensible or pragmatic to preserve the strict equality rule. All eligible adults should receive the same amount, with additional separate benefits for those with disabilities, bearing in mind their special needs and reduced opportunity income.

One view is that the basic income should vary according to regional costs of living and average incomes, so that a lower amount would be paid in poorer regions. This is unlikely to be relevant in the design of pilots. But at national level, the main drawback of such an approach is that it would entrench or worsen inter-regional income inequalities. If the basic income were paid equally, it would represent a higher amount in lower-income regions, and thus be a mechanism for reducing inter-area and interpersonal income inequality. It might even be a factor leading to shifts of investment and population to lower-income areas, giving a further boost to their local economies.

Serious advocates of moving in the direction of a basic income do not see it as a panacea.[1] It will not 'abolish poverty' or 'abolish unemployment'. It will not provide perfect freedom or perfect basic security. But it will enhance freedom and strengthen security. It must be seen as part of a new income distribution system suited to a globalizing open economy, and as part of a transformative policy package, along with new forms of collective representation and ownership. The socially and economically vulnerable will always remain that way in the absence of collective Voice. A basic income should help in strengthening such Voice, or agency. But nobody should think it could do that optimally without measures to build and strengthen modern forms of unionism. The libertarian or neoliberal paradigm should be rejected with confidence that enough people will understand the need for a strong social state.

It is also vital to emphasize that a basic income system would enhance the prospects of a more ecologically and socially sustainable form of 'growth', elevating the value of care work, community work and participation in the life of the commons, and allowing government to pursue more effective fiscal policies to curb greenhouse gas emissions. It would also do better than any alternative in enhancing basic economic security, personal and 'republican' freedom, and social justice.

In all these respects, moving in the direction of a basic income or common dividends would be transformative. Not only would it give an anchor to that new distribution system, in a context of stagnant, increasingly volatile and uncertain real wages, it would also encourage work that is not paid labour and social solidarity instead of utilitarian individualism, which a regime of means-testing, behaviour-testing and workfare inevitably fosters.

In seeking to build a more progressive income distribution system, there are two starkly different directions in which social policy could go. One is to continue in the direction taken by Universal Credit, which will mean more means-testing, more behaviour-testing, more sanctions, more intrusive directions that deliberately limit the freedom of lower-income citizens. This is the utilitarian direction. It will strengthen the giants of inequality, insecurity, debt, stress and precarity.

The alternative direction is one that would give equal freedom to all, with more trust and less direction and coercion directed to the vulnerable. That way would lead to a steady weakening of those giants. The distribution system that would take shape could have an anchor or base with common dividends and second tiers of other forms of income transfer, through social insurance, private insurance and needs-based supplements. We need to rebuild the welfare state on new universalistic principles.

It is the direction that matters above all, even with a modest start. A survey conducted by Nationwide in 2018 revealed that a third of people privately renting in the UK – millions of people – after paying their rent, their gas and electricity and food, had only £23 to spend on everything else each week.[2] For those of our fellow citizens, even a low basic income would be enormously welcome.

Moving towards a system in which basic income or common dividends is an integral part would be a radical return to Britain's great progressive traditions. Our progressive journey has been marked by successive waves of emancipation and democratization, triumphing despite eras of retreat and defeat. Giving ordinary people greater control over their own lives and the lives of their families and communities is central to the progressive journey. Moving towards a basic income as a right to subsistence, a right to a home and a right to work will be part of the renewal of the Enlightenment values of equality, liberty and solidarity. It is vital for all those on the 'left' to couch social policy in those terms.

Finally, to reiterate a point made earlier, Conservative governments, and some previous Labour governments, have used the power of the state to control people's lives – treating lower-income individuals and families as supplicants to be reformed or 'sanctioned'. A progressive government should use the power of the state to empower people, to have agency and greater security and control over their own lives and an ability to forge communities of their own volition. A basic income would help in doing just that.

Appendix A:
Experience with pilots

Contrary to claims by some critics that there is no evidence on the impact of basic income, a series of experiments have yielded relevant findings.[1] While most have not been complete basic income pilots, most have been flagged as testing basic income and have important features of a proper basic income, such as non-conditionality.

(1) Manitoba-Mincome

Although there were negative income tax (NIT) experiments in the United States in the 1970s, the first pilot in the spirit of basic income was launched in 1975 in the province of Manitoba, Canada, which included a 'saturation' variant in Dauphin, a small town. The Manitoba Basic Annual Income Experiment (Mincome) is also notorious for the fact that, after it was ended prematurely due to a change of government, all the evaluation data were lost. Nearly 40 years later, they were discovered in the national archives in 1,800 dusty boxes.

The payments were targeted at recipients having an income below a pre-specified threshold, so this was not a true basic income experiment. However, analysis of the data clearly showed that receiving a guaranteed income led to improved health, with fewer hospital visits, accidents and injuries, including from domestic violence, and a considerable 'reduction in physician claims for mental health disorders'. This suggested that basic income would 'improve health and social outcomes at the community level'.[2] There was also a peer-group effect in education. Youths in recipient families, especially boys, were less likely to drop out of high school following introduction of the guaranteed income – but so were their classmates from non-recipient families. Recipients felt a greater sense of economic security and the scheme de-stigmatized income assistance, because it was seen as for everybody.[3] This contrasts with the impact of means-testing as the existing core of the British welfare system. The community-level benefits demonstrate the desirability of designing British basic income pilots to cover everyone in a community rather than just a sample of individuals. Spill-over and communal effects matter.

(2)   North Carolina

An important 'accidental pilot' occurred in North Carolina, although it is non-replicable. Shortly after the launch of a long-term longitudinal study of child development in the area, a Native American community decided to convert the profits of the local casino into basic income payments for community members. This enabled researchers to compare outcomes for affected children against those for others in the study. Children in families receiving the basic income did much better in school than those in the control group, and there was a 'dramatic decrease' in juvenile crime. The researchers attributed these findings largely to better family relations because parents were under less stress from economic insecurity.

Although 'casino dividend' schemes, of which there are several in North America, are scarcely replicable for British purposes, this study shows that long-term feedback effects should be taken into account in any sensible modelling of the effects of a basic income. Critics have singularly failed to do so.

(3)   Alaska Permanent Fund

Alaska has a common-dividend-type scheme, which is often lauded as 'the most popular program in the history of the US'.[4] The Alaska Permanent Fund was set up in 1976 by the maverick Republican state governor with royalties from the oil industry. It began issuing dividends to all state residents in 1982, on an individual basis, and is still going today. By 2018, the fund was worth 113% of Alaska's GDP, and over the years its diversified portfolio yielded annual returns of nearly 10%.[5] Anything like that from a Commons Fund in the UK would make a decent basic income eminently affordable within the lifetime of a single parliament. Dividends from the Alaska fund have reduced poverty and economic insecurity. They have also been associated with increased employment and improved schooling attainment by disadvantaged youth.

Unsurprisingly, the fund and dividends have been very popular with state residents. In 2018 the governor, elected as an independent, was forced to withdraw from his re-election campaign after cutting the dividend and proposing to raid the fund for public spending. The state abolished income tax when oil revenues were high and the cut in dividends was correctly seen as a tax on low-income Alaskans. Whereas the fund itself is protected by a constitutional amendment, the payment of dividends is not, allowing some unprincipled political meddling. This failing should be avoided in any British move.

The fund and dividend model is replicable and upscalable. It is also affordable and politically feasible. And, unlike almost every other quasi-basic income scheme, it is permanent. Its limitations are that the amount is paid only once a year as a lump sum, and it is a variable rather than a predictable amount, depending on the annual returns to the fund.

Norway built up its permanent capital fund by retaining ownership of its share of North Sea oil. Today it is the world's biggest capital fund.

Had the UK pursued the same North Sea oil strategy as Norway, it would have had an even bigger fund by now, which could easily have funded a generous basic income. That was one of the several missed chances to create such a fund, using the proceeds of sales of public assets. But a British government could still build up a national capital fund from levies on commercial uses of the commons.[6] The ethical, moral and economic case for doing so is strong.

(4)   Namibia, India and Kenya

A few years ago, it was largely presumed that a basic income system could not be introduced in any low-income developing country. In the past decade, this view has been disproved. There have been many conditional cash transfer schemes, particularly in Latin America, and an increasing number of *unconditional* cash transfer schemes. Most of these have been targeted on the poor via means-tests or proxy means-tests, but increasingly the evidence has accumulated that quasi-universal schemes function more efficiently and equitably.[7]

There have been several pilots of basic income in developing countries, the first being in Namibia, where a modest basic income was given to all residents of a small village. Although no control group was used, in most respects the results matched those from the much bigger pilots launched in Madhya Pradesh, India, which covered about 6,000 men, women and children. The basic income was universal, given to every usual resident of eight villages for 18 months. Outcomes were matched with a control group of every resident in twelve otherwise similar villages.

The methodology used in the Indian pilot is replicable and could be a model for any British pilot. A baseline survey was undertaken before the pilot was announced and the recipient villages identified; this was effectively a census, covering all households. Then there was an interim evaluation survey conducted about six months after the start of the pilot and a final evaluation survey conducted at the end of the period. A novel feature was that, three years after the pilot was concluded, a legacy survey was carried out. This was designed to identify what effects of the pilot had continued after it ended, and what changes had not lasted.

Analysis of the evaluation data, the data from 'key informants' and the detailed case studies, indicated that the basic incomes resulted in improved health, nutrition, sanitation, schooling and economic activity, with several indicators of a strong emancipatory effect for women, the disabled and minorities.[8] There was also evidence that the universality of the basic income system induced feelings of social solidarity and the emergence of stronger local governance and local cooperatives.

The biggest basic income pilot launched so far is taking place in Kenya, funded and implemented by GiveDirectly, a US-based non-profit organization. One of the three variants it is testing involves the provision of a modest basic income to 21,000 villagers for a period of 12 years. While this pilot has generated a lot of international publicity, it will take a long time before evaluations begin to emerge, during which time there is likely to be considerable research fatigue and staff turnover. And one would hope for policy implementation long before it ends.

The survey instruments developed for the Indian pilots, in particular, are easily adaptable to British conditions. Their availability would reduce time and costs. In demanding 'evidence-based policy-making', it is often insufficiently appreciated that specifying hypotheses by which to judge success or failure is complex, requiring appropriate data collection.

In January 2019, citing the results of the pilots, the Indian Congress Party, one of the largest political movements in the world, announced that if elected in the forthcoming General Election it would introduce a basic income 'for the bottom half of the income distribution'. This dramatically helped to legitimize basic income in the mainstream political discourse. Almost immediately, the BJP governing party included a scheme of its own in the manifesto for the April–May General Election, in which it won an overwhelming victory, and several state governments announced they would introduce schemes that would be even closer to a basic income.

(5) The Great British Benefits Handout

In 2017, Dragonfly, a documentary film company, made a six-part TV series, *The Great British Benefits Handout*, in which a few families, all receiving benefits, were given the equivalent of one year's benefits in a lump sum, amounting to £23,000 per family, without conditions. The families were then followed to see how the money was used and what impact it had on their lives.

This was a capital grant scheme rather than a proper basic income or social dividend scheme, and there was therefore the risk that people would squander or misuse the money ('weakness of will' effects). However, it proved remarkably successful. All the families used the money to improve living standards and do more work, paid and unpaid.

The DWP allowed this experiment to take place, indicating that such experiments are administratively feasible. *The Times*, reviewing the series, said that the DWP secretary of state should be required to watch and learn from it. There is no evidence that he or his successors did so.

(6) The City of London Homelessness Project

In an intriguing experiment in central London, a small number of individuals who had been sleeping rough for between four months and 45 years were asked what they thought they needed to get off the streets. They were then given the cash to do so, averaging £3,000 each, with varying levels of voluntary engagement with support workers. By the end of the experiment, the majority were in accommodation or planned to move into somewhere soon.[9] Helping the homeless in this way turned out to cost much less than existing provision, since rough sleepers are often hospitalized and frequently end up in prison.

This experiment is clearly replicable, but it may not be upscalable to regional or national level. Some people might deliberately become homeless in order to obtain the grant and extra help. However, such was the success of the first experiment of this type that similar experiments should be undertaken in another part of the country with high levels of homelessness. The idea would be to determine whether such a policy should figure in the political response to one of the worst outcomes of austerity.

(7) Finland

Despite its billing in the press, the Finnish experiment was not really a basic income pilot, even though it may prove useful in furthering policy development in that direction. The originators had wished to test a basic income, applied to whole communities and every resident, regardless of work status. However, this was whittled down by political and budgetary pressures. Instead, a basic income of €560 a month was provided to 2,000 randomly selected unemployed people between January 2017 and December 2018, with no conditions attached and no withdrawal if they found jobs in that period. To help obtain political support for the pilot, it was stated before it began that 'the primary goal' was 'promoting employment', which most advocates of basic income would not regard as a desirable indicator of 'success'.[10]

At the time of writing, it is not possible to say definitively what the outcomes have been, although evaluation of data began in late 2018. But it at least seems to have resulted in reduced stress and improved attitudes to work and job-seeking. A preliminary official analysis issued in February 2019 concluded that the payments had not produced any decline in employment – indeed, there was tentative evidence that recipients had half a day more in employment – and it had resulted in significant improvements in well-being, with a 17% incidence of better physical and mental health, and a 37% decrease in the incidence of depression.[11]

Making that result more impressive was the fact that the employment rate was no higher in the control group, even though an 'activation' scheme had been introduced by the centre-right government halfway through the pilot that sanctioned unemployed people by reducing their benefits if they did not pursue or obtain jobs. The fact that the employment rates of the basic income recipients were the same as for those threatened with punitive sanctions shows that sanctions are unnecessary.[12]

An interview with one of the previously unemployed recipients of the basic income reported that he had used the time and money to build up a workshop for making and selling shaman drums.[13] However, it was not the money that had made that possible but the absence of behavioural conditions that had previously forced him to look for jobs and use up time to satisfy the employment bureau's demands.

An artist who had also been one of the basic income recipients, who came to the annual congress of the Basic Income Earth Network (BIEN) held in Tampere, Finland, in August 2018, said in a statement: 'We are all emotional beings as well as rational ones. My basic income payment was the day I became free – a signal I could dream of something better.' Other recipients reported that it had encouraged them to be more entrepreneurial.[14]

In November 2018, the opposition party, Left Alliance, announced that its manifesto for the General Election scheduled for 2019 would include a commitment to a basic income of €800 a month, phasing out means-tested social assistance, while leaving housing allowance unchanged. The basic income would be 'taxed away' from high-income earners, and it would be phased in by consolidating various social security benefits.

The pilot in Finland should not be taken as an exemplary test of a basic income, only of labour supply and well-being effects of moving in that direction. Advocates and critics alike should be cautious about interpreting the outcomes. Suppose, for example, that the final evaluation shows a small decline in labour supply but improvements in mental health. How should the 'success' of the pilot be judged?

(8) Ontario

In April 2017, the provincial government of Ontario, Canada, launched a basic income pilot covering three areas – Hamilton, Lindsay and Thunder Bay – where samples were selected. The scheme enrolled 4,000 low-income individuals in the three areas, paying single people about C$17,000 a year and couples C$24,000. People with disabilities were given a supplement.

The scheme was closer to a negative income tax experiment, since the basic income was reduced by 50 cents for every extra dollar earned, and it was household-based rather than paid individually. But given those limitations the experiment began well. However, it was cancelled by the new right-wing government on taking office in August 2018, reversing an election pledge to let it continue to completion.[15] The suspension led to widespread public protest.

In the few months the Ontario pilots were allowed to operate, initial reports were encouraging.[16] It is hoped that a similar pilot planned in British Columbia will not have a similar fate. In the Ontario pilot, a baseline survey was conducted and a baseline report prepared. But the pilot was cancelled before a first follow-up survey could be carried out. Moreover, the new provincial government instructed the evaluation team to return all documentation, thereby preventing the public from finding out how the pilots were working.

Since participants had made financial and other commitments on the assumption that they would receive the basic income payments for 18 months more, the government extended payment of the stipends until March 2019. But no further data were collected. Nevertheless, an unofficial survey of participants found that there had been a substantial increase in voluntary work, while 88% of recipients felt less stressed.

(9) The Netherlands

Following legislation in 2015 allowing local authorities to experiment with social policies, several Dutch cities launched schemes involving variations of basic income. By 2018, partial basic income pilots were underway in Groningen, Tilburg, Utrecht and Wageningen. The payments are limited to welfare claimants, with people randomly selected and assigned to be a recipient or to be in the control group.[17]

Interest in these pilots lies primarily in the fact that they are testing for the effects of relaxing conditionalities in connection with so-called active labour market policies and will allow recipients to keep some of the benefit as they earn. Results will not emerge until late 2019. One early conclusion, however, is that scope for local variants of basic income pilots should be allowed and incorporated into any proposed British pilot programme, to broaden the evidence base.

(10) California

One much-reported pilot has been hatched in California, funded by Y-Combinator Research and run by tech entrepreneurs. The original plan was to give a sample of people in the city of Oakland $1,000 a month. But after three years of preparatory work, its project director announced that it would not be conducted in Oakland after all but in two regions in two states. The current plan is to give unconditional cash transfers of $1,000 per month to 1,000 people and $50 to a control group of 2,000 to compensate them for their cooperation in filling in questionnaires. Some participants will receive their basic income for three years, some for five. The study is now called 'Making Ends Meet'.

One problem the designers have had to overcome is the need to obtain official permission in order to ensure that participants are not made worse off by the withdrawal of existing benefits. The lesson is that any pilot has to have the backing of all the relevant authorities from an early stage. A positive outcome so far is that the very existence of the project has helped legitimize basic income in the public policy debate in California and beyond to other parts of the United States. Another useful outcome of the protracted negotiations has been a technical guide to the conduct of basic income pilots in American cities.[18]

(11) Stockton, California and Elsewhere in the United States

The second California pilot is really a demonstration project rather than a scientific pilot. A new young mayor, Michael Tubbs, launched a basic income trial in February 2019, which gives 130 residents $500 a month for 18 months, with no restrictions on how the money can be spent or what the recipients do with their time. The programme, named the Stockton Economic Empowerment Demonstration (SEED), is being funded primarily by a $1 million grant from Chris Hughes, one of the co-founders of Facebook, and a further $2 million from foundations and individuals.

The 130 people provided with the basic income had to be at least 18 years old and live in a neighbourhood in the run-down city with an average income below the median for the city. The sample of 130 was selected randomly from applicants from a sample of 1,000 residences, all of whom were asked to indicate their interest in being included. A control group with a similar socio-economic background was also selected. Among the hypotheses to be tested mentioned by the mayor was that receipt of basic income would result in less street crime.

Mayor Tubbs seems to have his objectives quite clear, in saying,

> What's important is that people are suffering right now, today. The most important thing the pilot can do is spark a conversation that might translate down the road into state or nationwide change. The Stockton pilot is important because it shows that a local elected [person] can talk about this and not die for it. The public is actually ready for this conversation.

In another newspaper interview, Tubbs responded with exemplary compassion and empathy to being asked about the risk of the pilot failing:

> If we are saying that we trust people, then we actually have to trust them. The folks who are receiving the benefits are no different from you and I. I know sometimes I spend money in ways I shouldn't on things that are not necessities, but for the most part I make sure my basic needs are met first. I extend the same level of grace to those who are selected. I may not agree with every single way they spend their money, but if I can't trust my folks to make good decisions, why would I put my name on the ballot and ask them to trust me to be the mayor?[19]

Another quasi-basic income pilot is being launched in four American cities, in which 1,000 low-income mothers will be provided with an unconditional $333 per month, with a control group being provided with $20 per month, the money to be put on a prepaid debit card on the date of the child's birthday for 40 consecutive months. The study is called 'Baby's First Years', because the focus is on the expected link between basic income security in early life and brain development.

The primary hypothesis is that the steady stream of income will make a difference to the cognitive and emotional development of the children whose mothers receive it.

A professor of neuroscience connected to the project who has been studying the links for over 15 years wrote, 'Cash transfers, as opposed to counseling, child care and other services, have the potential to empower families to make the financial decisions they deem best for themselves and their children.'[20] Again, the project took a long time to be developed, mainly because the project team had to raise the funds and obtain approval for it through new legislation in the two states where it is being conducted.

Another small demonstration project is being conducted in Jackson, Mississippi, where 20 families have each been receiving $1,000 a month for 12 months. The sample was selected by a lottery, and initial results have been encouraging.[21]

Finally, Chicago is considering a basic income pilot which, if it takes off, will be the largest pilot in the United States so far. The plan is to provide 1,000 low-income individuals with $1,000 per month for 18 months. The chair of the taskforce recommending the pilot, Alderman Ameya Pawar, said his hope was 'to help the poor from becoming the hopeless'. Shortly afterwards, the Mayor of Newark, New Jersey, in his State of the City Address, announced that his city too would be piloting a basic income.

Local demonstration projects of these types, including some financed by private donors, should be encouraged and facilitated in areas of Britain where more scientific pilots are not being implemented.

(12) Barcelona: B-Mincome

One of the more interesting pilots underway is Barcelona's B-Mincome, which began in October 2017 and is scheduled to last two years. This has 1,000 participant families, plus 500 as a control group, which is probably too small a sample, given the 11 variants being tested. It is also not really a test of basic income, being family-based and more like a negative income tax. However, the experiment has helped to legitimize the idea of basic income across the region. When launched, it was stated that the main intention was 'to analyse the most effective way of reducing inequality and breaking the poverty cycle'.

(13)   Germany: HartzPlus

Finally, in Germany, a privately funded basic income pilot – named provocatively *HartzPlus* after Hartz IV, the controversial welfare reform introduced in 2005 – started in May 2019 in Berlin. A random sample of 250 recipients of state benefits will be paid €416 a month for three years, with another 250 acting as a control group. The focus is on evaluating the impact on labour market behaviour, health and social relations. The pilot follows crowd-funded schemes that have proved popular in Germany, notably *Mein Grundeinkommen* ('My Basic Income') that runs a lottery that gives winners a monthly basic income of €1,000 for one year. Meanwhile, the chief executive of Germany's Association of Towns and Municipalities, lamenting the over-burdened bureaucratic welfare state and rising poverty, has come out in favour of basic income.

Appendix B:
Why a job guarantee would
be no alternative

The claim made in this book is that a basic income would promote social justice, freedom and basic security while combating the eight giants, in ways that other possible policies would not. Among the policies advocated as alternatives is a job guarantee for everyone, or for everyone 'able to work'.[1] In the United States, several prominent Democrat senators and possible candidates for the 2020 presidential election have said they support the idea, including Bernie Sanders, Cory Booker, Elizabeth Warren, Kamala Harris and Kirsten Gillibrand. In Britain *The Guardian* has endorsed it unequivocally as 'a welcome return to a politics of work'.[2]

The Guardian claimed that a job guarantee policy 'would secure a basic human right to engage in productive employment'. Throughout history, the vast majority of people would have found that a very strange 'human right'.[3] Having a job is to be in a position of subordination, reporting to and obeying a boss in return for payment. Indeed, historically the words 'job', 'jobbing' and 'jobholder' were terms of regret and even pity, referring to someone with a bits-and-pieces existence. Subordination and alienation have also been at the heart of labour law, which is based on the master–servant model.

The newspaper added that the job guarantee 'would only offer employment under-supplied by the private sector', singling out 'environmental clean-up' and 'social care'. These may sound appealing on paper but represent a narrow and unattractive range of jobs to be offered. They also bear more than a passing resemblance to the menial jobs convicted offenders are obliged to undertake under 'community payback' schemes.

The practical objections become evident as soon as the details are considered: What jobs would be offered, who would be responsible for providing them, who would qualify to be offered them, what would the jobs pay and for how many hours, who would pay, how much would it cost to supervise participants and to police compliance with the job's requirements, and what would be the effects on other workers and on the wider economy?

To start with, identifying jobs to be provided and administering the process would be a bureaucratic nightmare (witness the shambles of many 'community payback' schemes, even though they are on a small scale and the labour they offer is 'free'). And, when asked what type of job would be guaranteed, proponents never suggest that the guaranteed jobs would match people's skills and qualifications, instead falling back on low-skill, low-wage jobs they would not dream of for themselves or their children.

Then other questions arise. If guaranteed jobs are providing desired services or goods, and are subsidized, there must be substitution effects – guaranteeing jobs now taken by others – and deadweight effects – putting people in jobs that would have been created anyhow. If somebody is given a guaranteed job at the minimum wage, what happens to others already doing such jobs? Would the job guarantee agency guarantee their jobs as well, with no decline in wages if they happened to be higher? If the unemployed were offered a job at a minimum wage subsidized by the state, this would increase the vulnerability of others, either displacing them or lowering their income.

Moreover, guaranteed jobs may displace better jobs, if only because public sector managers would have an incentive to hire those workers with guaranteed jobs at lower wages and worse working conditions. The job guarantee scheme would thereby put downward pressure on the wages and working conditions of middle-income jobs.[4]

Ro Khanna, a California Democrat congressman, has said firms would not be allowed to hire subsidized workers if they were substitutes for previous employees.[5] Clever employers could find ways round that. However, it would also be unfair. Why should a firm coming into a market be subsidized relative to one that has been in it for a while, giving the newcomer an unfair advantage?

The Guardian further claimed, without citing evidence, that a job guarantee scheme would not be inflationary because 'any restructuring of relative wages would be a one-off event'. This contradicts generations of research. If all were guaranteed a job, what would stop wage-push inflation? The only restraining factors would be fear of automation and more offshoring. But it would hardly be fear, as a job would be guaranteed anyhow!

The gross cost of a job guarantee might outweigh the net gain. If the government guaranteed the minimum wage in guaranteed jobs, those in jobs paying less (or working fewer than the guaranteed hours) might quit or find ways to be made redundant, so they could have a guaranteed job instead. Social democrats might like that, as it would mean better-paying jobs for more of the underemployed and precariat. But the fiscal cost would be daunting. For example, in the UK, over 60% of those regarded as poor are in jobs or have someone in their household who is.[6] Would they all become eligible for a guaranteed good job?

At its unlikely best, a job guarantee would be paternalistic. It presumes the government knows what is best for individuals, who would be offered a necessarily limited range of jobs at its disposal. Suppose someone was pressed to take a guaranteed job on a construction site ('infrastructure', a favoured area for guaranteed jobs) and that person proved incompetent and was injured. Would the job guarantee agency be held responsible and pay compensation? It should, since it put the person in that position. How would that be factored into the costing of a job guarantee scheme? Similarly, if a person put into a 'social care' job was negligent and caused harm or distress to the care recipient, would the latter be able to sue the job guarantee agency for compensation?

In addition, a job guarantee scheme would spring a familiar trap – the phoney distinction between those who 'can work' and would thus be eligible for a guaranteed job and those 'who cannot work'.[7] In Britain, this has led to the demeaning and stigmatizing 'capacity-to-work' and 'availability-for-work' tests, resulting in more discriminatory action against disabled and vulnerable people, and those with care responsibilities.

Another failing of the job guarantee route is the mapping of a path to 'workfare'. What would happen to somebody who declined to accept the guaranteed job? They would be labelled 'lazy' or 'choosy' and thus 'ungrateful' and 'socially irresponsible'. Yet there are many reasons for refusing a job. Studies show that accepting a job below a person's qualifications can lower their income and social status for the long term. As what is happening in the current UK benefit system attests, those not taking jobs allocated to them would face benefit sanctions, and be directed into jobs, whether they liked them or not. Jobs done in resentment or under duress are unlikely to be done well.

A job guarantee would be a recipe for perpetuating low productivity. What would happen if a person in a guaranteed job performed poorly, perhaps because of limited ability or simply because they knew it was 'guaranteed'? If you are guaranteed a job, why bother to work hard? If you are an employer and are given a subsidy to pay employees guaranteed a job, why bother to try to use labour efficiently?

If subsidized through tax credits or a wage subsidy, a worker would need to produce only a little more value than the cost to the employer to make it profitable to retain him or her. This would cheapen low-productivity jobs relative to others and inhibit the higher productivity arising from labour-displacing technological change. If a job of a certain type is guaranteed, what happens if an employer wishes to invest in technology that would remove the need for such jobs?

Those calling for a job guarantee also ignore the fact that any market economy requires some unemployment, as people need time to search for jobs they are prepared to accept, and firms must sift applicants for jobs they want to have done. To adopt a job guarantee policy would risk putting the economy in gridlock.

Job guarantee advocates, such as Larry Summers, President Clinton's former treasury secretary, argue that people without jobs 'are much more likely to be dissatisfied with their lives' and are more likely to be drug addicts and abusive than those with even low-wage jobs.[8] This is bogus. I suggest there would be no correlation between life satisfaction and having a job if the comparison was made between those in lousy jobs and those with no job but an adequate income on which to live. Somebody facing a choice between penury and a lousy job will prefer the job. But that does not mean they like or want it for itself.

The polling company Gallup conducts regular *State of the Global Workplace* surveys in over 150 countries. In 2017, it found that globally only 15% of workers were engaged by their job, and in no country did the figure exceed 40%. One recent UK survey found that 37% of jobholders did not think their job made any significant contribution.

Summers ends his article by equivocating that 'the idea of a jobs guarantee should be taken seriously but not literally.' He seems to mean government should try to promote more employment, through 'wage subsidies, targeted government spending, support for workers with dependants, and more training and job-matching programs'. In other words, he reverts to the standard social democratic package that has not done very well in the past three decades.

Besides being a recipe for labour inefficiency and labour market distortions, tending to displace workers employed in the 'free' labour market and to depress their wages, the job guarantee proposal fails to recognize that today's crisis is structural and requires transformative policies. Tax credits, job guarantees and statutory minimum wages would barely touch the precariat's existential insecurity that is at the heart of the social and economic crisis, let alone address the aspirations of the progressive and growing part of the precariat for an ecologically grounded Good Society.[9]

The emphasis on jobs is non-ecological, since it is tied to the constant pursuit of economic growth. There are many instances, support for fracking and for the third runway at Heathrow airport being recent examples, where the promise of more jobs has trumped costs to health and the environment. And a job guarantee policy could have a strong appeal to the political right as a way to dismantle the welfare state. Why pay unemployment benefits if everybody has a guaranteed job? In the United States, one conservative commentator chortled that 'over 100 federal welfare programs would be replaced with a single job guarantee program'.[10]

Finally, there is what this writer regards as the policy's worst feature. It would reinforce twentieth-century labourism, by failing to make the distinction between work and labour. Those who back guaranteed jobs typically ignore all forms of work that are not paid labour. A really progressive agenda would strengthen the values of work over the dictates of labour. It would seek to enable more people to develop their own sense of occupation.[11]

A job is a means to an end, not an end in itself. Economists tend to be inconsistent in this respect. In the textbooks, labour has 'disutility'; it is negative for the worker. Yet many economists who use or write these textbooks then advocate putting everybody in jobs. Why make a fetish of 'jobs'? A job is doing 'labour' for others. What about all the forms of work that we do for those we love or for our community or for ourselves?

Many forms of work that are not labour are more rewarding psychologically and socially. A regime of putting everybody into jobs, in unchosen activities, would be orchestrated alienation. Surely a progressive should want to minimize the time we spend in stultifying and subordinated jobs, so that we can increase the time and energy for forms of work and leisure that are self-chosen and oriented to personal and community development.

There is one last point, to do with the claim that a job guarantee would be politically popular. Much is made of a US poll which asked people whether they would support a scheme to guarantee a job for anybody 'who can't find employment in the private sector', if paid from a 5% tax on those earning over $200,000. The result was 52% in favour. Supporters thought this was 'stunning'.[12] With such a loaded question, one should be stunned by the bare-majority support. After all, most respondents were being told they would not have to pay, and that there were no alternative jobs available, an unlikely scenario.

Rather than jobs per se, the primary challenge is to build a new income distribution system, recognizing that the old one has broken down irretrievably. The rentiers are running away with all the revenue thrown up by rentier capitalism, and real wages will continue to lag. Putting people into static low-wage jobs is no response.

Appendix C:
Why 'universal basic services' would be no alternative

Free 'universal basic services' (UBS) has recently been advocated as a better alternative to a basic income,[1] on the grounds that it would be a cheaper and more cost-effective way of combating poverty.[2] On the premise that 'essential services should be free at the point of need', paralleling the National Health Service and state education, proponents have identified universal free 'basic' housing, free food, free local transport, free TV licence and a free 'basic' communications package including mobile phone and broadband internet. All of this, they claim, would cost £42 billion or about 2.3% of GDP.[3]

We should be united in wanting more and better public services. But improving public services is not in opposition to providing a basic income. They would fulfil different needs and purposes. However, the proposals for UBS are not what they seem at first sight.

For a start, what is being proposed is not 'universal' in any accepted use of the word.[4] For instance, the provision of 'free food' under the UBS banner is deceptive. According to the UBS scheme, the state would provide 'one-third of the meals for the 2.2 million households deemed to experience food insecurity each year'.[5] That is not universal. It is targeted. Identifying those suffering from food insecurity would necessarily imply means-testing or some complex test of 'food insecurity'. As with all targeted schemes, many of those eligible would not be reached, while those receiving the free food would, as a result, face an even greater poverty trap and accompanying precarity trap than exist in the British welfare state today.[6]

The proposal would also generate a new moral hazard. Someone deemed food insecure, and thus entitled to free meals, would have a disincentive to become food secure, unless the free food on offer were lousy (which could hardly be a policy objective, even though it is likely to be a policy outcome). That moral hazard would be accompanied by an equally perverse 'immoral' hazard, since some people would have an incentive to become food insecure deliberately in order to claim free meals.[7]

Providing 'the poor' with free food would extend the charity state and institutionalize the obnoxious system of food banks, which have mushroomed in the austerity era. The mass provision of free food would also risk more waste of food. However well intentioned the charity state might be, people receiving free goods tend to value them less and treat them with less care than if they pay for them.

In practice, the choice of what food to make free would be arbitrary, based on paternalistic views of what is good for 'the poor' and what is not. Those countries that have implemented highly subsidized food have not had great success with it. And there is the likely effect of stigmatization of food support claimants, as has been the case with food stamps in the United States. Many are so ashamed to show their poverty that they forego their entitlement.

The next UBS on the advocates' list is free basic housing. That would not be a 'universal' service either, since it would be 'offered on a needs basis'. All the problems related to targeted provision of free food would apply here too. How would 'need' be determined without a means-test? What would happen if people no longer 'needed' the basic housing – would they be evicted? Incentives to become 'in need' to qualify for free housing would be enormous, unless the 'basic' housing was so unattractive as to weed out all but the truly desperate, *increasing* their marginalization in new 'sink estates'.

Perhaps unsurprisingly, in the latest advocacy of UBS, 'universal' free food and free housing are not mentioned at all, while free childcare and adult social care make an appearance instead.[8] So, in this manifestation, two of the most basic of needs – food and shelter – are effectively regarded as not basic. And as free childcare and adult social care were not costed by the original report proposing UBS, £42 billion is likely to be a considerable underestimate. With the added services, UBS would surely be a good deal more expensive than its proponents claim.

The latest report on UBS cites an estimate of £33 billion (1.8% of GDP) for the gross cost of providing free childcare, with workers providing it paid the minimum wage. The cost is then finessed down to a lowly £1.7 billion by assuming employment gains, higher tax receipts and reduced income support payments. But in a sleight of hand, in asserting that UBS would cost much less than basic income, UBS proponents cite only what they claim would be the gross cost of a basic income, not a net cost. Yet the difference between gross and net costs could be expected to be even larger in the case of basic income since, apart from savings in benefit expenditure, the basic income would effectively be clawed back from those on higher incomes through the tax system.

As for eldercare, the report omits to put a figure on its cost. However, a report on funding adult social care, issued jointly by two House of Commons committees, cites an estimate of £14 billion annually to make personal care services in England free of charge to all; they are already free in Scotland. An additional £15 billion would be needed just to restore services to their pre-austerity levels.[9]

A more recent estimate by the Institute for Public Policy Research (IPPR) has put the cost of free personal care in England at £8 billion over and above the £28 billion needed by 2030 for the present inadequate system to keep pace with demand, against about £19 billion today.[10] While there would be some offsetting savings to the NHS, the IPPR envisages a 2p rise in the basic rate of income tax to finance the proposal.

None of this is to argue against better quality provision and affordable access to child and eldercare, both of which are sorely needed. But they are not cheap options and may even be regressive, benefiting the well-off most, depending on how they are funded. Meanwhile, the paternalist emphasis by proponents of UBS on free state provision risks neglecting those who provide informal care for their own relations and those who try to stay independent of care for as long as possible. According to the House of Commons report, unpaid carers provide an estimated £132 billion-worth of care each year.[11]

Interestingly, under the German social care scheme, admired by both the House of Commons committees and UBS supporters, three quarters of beneficiaries opt for cash payments, even though they are lower than the value of the free in-kind services offered, because cash payments give them the flexibility to be cared for at home by family members or other informal carers.[12]

This is exactly what supporters of a basic income envisage in supplementing the basic income for those with special needs due to disability or frailty. And a basic income for all could be expected to reduce the incidence of morbidity among the growing population of elderly and so promote more healthy active ageing, as well as facilitate more care work by those wishing to provide it to those they love.[13]

Then we come to the UBS advocates' proposal for free local transport. Once again, this is also not universal in any sense. It refers only to buses, which is hard luck on users of trains and metro systems, not to mention the many people living in areas with no or poor bus services.

While free bus services are popular, free bus rides are not like free health care or free education. Not everybody wants or needs to take buses. And free services may induce excessive or frivolous use. Buses also cause pollution. In rural areas, where the alternative may be the private car, a shift to buses could reduce pollution. But in cities it could encourage people to take the bus rather than use non-polluting alternatives, such as bicycling, walking or staying at home.

Privatization and cuts in government funding for local authorities, which have led to drastic reductions in subsidies for unprofitable bus services, means there are now few places in Britain with reliable bus services. A leading proponent of UBS claims that 'Public services offer security through the very fact that they offer greater permanence than money alone could ever provide.'[14] The fact is that over 3,000 bus routes have been axed in the past decade. What permanence? And, in an unintended consequence of free bus travel for the over-60s, these abandoned bus routes have included those once used predominantly by passengers with concessionary passes for which the bus operators argued they were not adequately compensated. Without investment in improving bus services, free travel for all could thus worsen services, rendering the benefit nugatory.

In addition, buses and other modes of public transport operate a hub-and-spoke model, whereas cars take people point-to-point. Free bus fares would benefit people, predominantly in urban areas, who live close to bus routes and need to travel to a hub such as the city centre. But they would do little or nothing for everyone else. In effect, their taxes would pay for others to benefit and, as with housing and food, the implied targeting might create resentment. A model of modest fares plus subsidies would ultimately be fairer, especially if there were a basic income.

So much for the limitations of what is actually proposed under UBS. But the proponents go further in provocatively presenting UBS as preferable to 'UBI' (Universal Basic Income).[15] Before considering this claim, I want to make clear that sensible advocates of basic income do not or should not use the word 'universal', because in practice some people would not be entitled to it – non-resident citizens and short-term or undocumented migrants. Presumably something similar would apply with UBS. That pragmatic matter aside, services and basic income have different objectives and justifications. Therefore, different criteria should be used to assess their desirability.

Anna Coote, principal fellow of the New Economics Foundation, dismisses basic income as 'snake oil'. So does Tom Kibasi, head of the social democratic IPPR, who indulges in more hyperbole in claiming it is an attempt to 'euthanise the working class as a concept'.[16]

Using the term 'snake oil' is an insulting way of accusing advocates of basic income of fraudulently selling the idea as a 'cure-all' when it is in fact useless. But progressive proponents of basic income make no claim that it could 'cure' anything. They do have considerable evidence that it has beneficial effects.[17]

As for accusations of euthanasia, that is a rather dramatic claim about an idea of providing everybody with basic income security. It recalls Lenin's reaction to seeing workers' allotments in Sweden on his way to Russia in 1917. He was against them because, he thought, having a plot of land would make people less likely to risk their lives in a revolution. The callousness of this posture is obvious.

Coote claims that UBS 'aims to tackle many of the challenges that advocates of UBI are trying to address'.[18] This is not true. For a start, advocates of basic income want to limit the paternalistic state, whereas UBS advocates want to extend it by pre-selecting what people need and, as in the case of food, extending conditionality and targeting. The basic income advocate says, 'I do not know what you need, but believe you should have the right to acquire it if you can'. The UBS advocate says, 'I know what you need, and I will make sure you can have it.'

A primary justification for moving towards an income distribution system in which a basic income is a core element is that the distribution system of the post-1945 era has broken down irretrievably. A new one suited to a global market economy, the ecological crisis, the ongoing technological revolution and changing household forms must be constructed in its place. A basic income, paid to individuals as a right, without means-tests or behavioural conditionalities, must be an anchor in that system. It is not a panacea; it is merely a necessary part of a progressive strategy, alongside a stronger social state.

Here, I want to reiterate that the principal reasons for wanting a basic income are ethical or moral, independent of its impact on poverty, inequality or the assumed threat to employment and incomes posed by automation and new technologies. Basic income is a matter of social justice, would enhance freedom and would give people basic security that would make them more altruistic, tolerant, cooperative and productive, as workers and as citizens. An income-insecure person with access to a free bus ride or even childcare or broadband would remain insecure.

Ultimately, there is no contradiction between having some public quasi-UBS and a basic income.[19] They address different needs and stem from different rationales. But having cash enhances freedom of choice, is potentially more empowering and can be more transformative. I plead with those advocating UBS to stop juxtaposing the idea of more and better public services with giving people basic income security.

Notes

Chapter 1

1 G. Standing, *Plunder of the Commons: A Manifesto for Sharing Public Wealth*, London: Pelican, 2019.

2 This was found in pilots in India. G. Standing, *Basic Income: And How We Can Make It Happen*, London: Pelican, 2017, pp. 65–7.

3 Contrary to some lurid press reports after the report for the Shadow Chancellor of the Exchequer was published, the basic income would not be banked for long-term convicted prisoners on release. Some advocates of basic income suggest payments to prisoners might be withheld. Another option would be to apply the basic income to offset prison accommodation costs.

4 C. Giles, 'Review: "Economics for the Many, edited by John McDonnell"', *Financial Times*, 24 September 2018.

5 P. Inman and R. Booth, 'Poverty Increases Among Children and Pensioners Across UK', *The Guardian*, 28 March 2019.

6 R. Joyce and X. Xu, *Inequalities in the Twenty-First Century: Introducing the IFS Deaton Review*, London: Institute for Fiscal Studies, May 2019, p. 5.

7 Editorial Board, 'Jobs Are No Longer a Route Out of Poverty in the UK', *Financial Times*, 23 May 2019.

8 C. Scott, J. Sutherland and A. Taylor, *Affordability of the UK's Eatwell Guide*, London: Food Foundation, September 2018.

9 Joseph Rowntree Foundation, *UK Poverty: Causes, Costs and Solutions*, London: Joseph Rowntree Foundation, September 2016.

10 P. Bourquin, J. Cribb, T. Waters and X. Xu, 'Why Has In-Work Poverty Risen in Britain', WP 19/12, Institute for Fiscal Studies, London, June 2019.

11 Editorial Board, 'Jobs Are No Longer a Route Out of Poverty in the UK'.

12 In the United States, 80% of those in jobs report having to live from week to week, without the ability to make savings.

13 F. Alvaredo, L. Chancel, T. Piketty, E. Saez and G. Zucman, *World Inequality Report 2018*, Cambridge, MA: Harvard University Press, 2018.

14 R. Neate, 'Hundreds Join Growing List of Britain's Ultra-Rich', *The Guardian*, 18 October 2018.

15 C. Bellfield, R. Blundell, J. Cribb, A. Hood and R. Joyce, 'Two Decades of Income Inequality in Britain: The Role of Wages, Household Earnings and Redistribution', Working Paper W17/01, Institute for Fiscal Studies, London, 2017, p. 6.

16 I owe this witty analogy to Danny Dorling. See also D. Dorling, 'Peak Inequality', *New Statesman*, 4 July 2018.

17 The exact wording is 'Percentiles 1-3 and 98-100 are excluded because of large statistical uncertainty.'

18 It is unclear to what extent the homeless are taken into account in measuring inequality.

19 G. Standing, *The Corruption of Capitalism: Why Rentiers Thrive and Work Does Not Pay*, London: Biteback, 2016.

20 B. Bell, P. Bukowski and S. Machlin, 'Rent Sharing and Inclusive Growth', DP13408, Centre for Economic Policy Research, London, December 2018.

21 See M. Simms and B. Hopkins, *Wage Inequality in the UK*, University of Leicester, October 2015.

22 The growing regional divide in incomes and wealth is not discussed here. It is an aspect of the growth of rentier capitalism and financialization, which has made London far wealthier than the rest of the country. N. Kommenda and L. Smears, 'Left Behind: How the Capital Has Pulled Away from the Rest of the UK', *The Guardian*, 6 May 2019, p. 7.

23 R. Blundell, R. Joyce, A. Norris-Keiller and J. P. Ziliak, 'Income Inequality and the Labour Market in Britain and the US', *Journal of Public Economics* 162, 2018, pp. 48–62.

24 *OECD Employment Outlook 2018*, Paris: OECD, 2018.

25 Bellfield et al., 'Two Decades of Income Inequality in Britain'.

26 G. Standing, *The Precariat: The New Dangerous Class*, London: Bloomsbury, 2011.

27 Department for Work and Pensions, *Households Below Average Income: An Analysis of the UK Income Distribution: 1994/95-2016/17*, London: HMSO, March 2018, p. 10.

28 See, for instance, S. Butler, 'Tesco Staff Get 10% Pay Rise – But Lose Their Annual Bonus', *The Guardian*, 11 June 2019, p. 30.

29 'Time to Perk Up', *The Economist*, 10 November 2018, p. 71.

30 F. McGuinness, 'Income Inequality in the UK', House of Commons Library Briefing Paper 7484, August 2018.

31 Standing, *Plunder of the Commons*.

32 Office for National Statistics, *Effects of Taxes and Benefits on UK Household Income: Financial Year Ending 2017*, London: HMSO, June 2018, p. 11.

33 'Graphic Detail: Tax and Inequality', *The Economist*, 13 April 2019, p. 77.

34 G. Bangham, 'How Wealthy Are You?', bbc.com, 1 July 2019, at https://www.bbc.com/news/uk-48759591

35 Alvaredo et al., *World Inequality Report 2018*, Figure E6.

36 C. Roberts and M. Lawrence, *Wealth in the Twenty-First Century*, London: IPPR, 2017.

37 G. Zucman, *The Hidden Wealth of Nations: The Scourge of Tax Havens*, Chicago: University of Chicago Press, 2016. Zucman estimated that hidden wealth has passed the $6 trillion mark.

38 A. Alstadsaeter, N. Johannesen and G. Zucman, 'Who Owns the Wealth in Tax Havens? Macro Evidence and Implications for Global Inequality', *Journal of Public Economics* 162, 2018, pp. 89–100.

39 Giles, 'Review: "Economics for the Many, edited by John McDonnell"'.

40 P. Collinson, 'Millennials Set to Reap Huge Rewards of Inheritance Boom', *The Guardian*, 29 December 2017.

41 OECD Statistics on Income Distribution and Poverty (database).

42 For a good review, see Psychologists for Social Change, *Universal Basic Income: A Psychological Impact Assessment*, London: Psychologists against Austerity, 2017.

43 Cited in L. Elliott, 'An Economic Recovery Based Around High Levels of Debt Is Really Not a Recovery at All', *The Guardian*, 17 September 2018, p. 25.

44 C. Barrett, 'Inside the UK's Debt Crisis', *Financial Times*, 26 April 2019.

45 R. Syal and R. Partington, 'Personal Debts "Shear Almost £900m off British Economy"', *The Guardian*, 6 September 2018.

46 R. Partington, 'UK Households Face Hidden Debt of Almost £19bn – Citizens Advice', *The Guardian*, 21 August 2018.

47 For a US view, see G. Rivlin, 'Confessions of a Payday Lender: "I Felt Like a Modern-Day Gangster"', *The Intercept*, 23 June 2016.

48 Citizens Advice, 'Harsh Collection Methods Adding Half a Billion in Fees to People's Council Tax Debt, Citizens Advice Reveals', Press Release, 26 April 2019.

49 P. Butler, 'Homeless People in UK "Denied Social Housing as Risky Tenants"', *The Guardian*, 15 May 2019.

50 R. Wilkinson and K. Pickett, *The Inner Level: How More Equal Societies Reduce Stress, Restore Sanity and Improve Everyone's Wellbeing*, London: Penguin, 2018.

51 Health and Safety Executive, 'Work Related Stress Depression or Anxiety Statistics in Great Britain, 2018', *HSE*, 31 October 2018.

52 M. Johnson, 'Universal Basic Income Can Directly Reduce Work-Related Stress', *Labourlist*, 20 August 2019.

53 S. Cohen, D. Janicki-Deverts, W. J. Doyle, G. E. Miller, E. Frank, B. S. Rabin and R. B. Turner, 'Chronic Stress, Glucocorticoid Receptor Resistance, Inflammation and Disease Risk', *Proceedings of the National Academy of Sciences* 109 (16), pp. 5995–9. I am grateful to Matthew Johnson for bringing my attention to this article.

54 Joyce and Xu, *Inequalities in the Twenty-First Century*, p. 8.

55 NHS Digital, 'Adult Psychiatric Morbidity Survey: Survey of Mental Health and Wellbeing, England, 2014', published online September 2016.

56 M. Johnson and E. Johnson, *The Health Case for Universal Basic Income*, Lancaster University, 2018.

57 S. Mullainathan and E. Shakir, *Scarcity: Why Having Too Little Means So Much*, London: Allen Lane, 2014; for further discussion of the link to basic income, see Standing, *Basic Income*, chapter 4.

58 E. A. Johnson and E. Spring, *The Activity Trap: Disabled People's Fear of Being Active*, Manchester: Activity Alliance, 2018.

59 D. Campbell, 'NHS Bosses: Benefit Stress Driving Mental Health Care Demand', *The Guardian*, 8 March 2019.

60 Standing, *The Precariat*.

61 See, for instance, OECD, *Automation, Skills and Training*, Paris: OECD, 2018.

62 World Economic Forum, *The Future of Jobs Report 2018*, Geneva: WEF, 2018.

63 The World Economic Forum has estimated that white-collar workers are among those most at risk of displacement.

64 A. Berg, E. F. Buffie and L.-F. Zanna, 'Should We Fear the Robot Revolution? (The Correct Answer Is Yes)', Working Paper 18/116, Washington DC: International Monetary Fund, May 2018.

65 J. Bughin and J. Manyika, 'Technology Convergence and AI Divides: A Simulation Appraisal', VoxEU.org, 7 September 2018.

66 C. Perez, *Technological Revolutions and Financial Capital: The Dynamics of Bubbles and Golden Ages*, Cheltenham: Edward Elgar, 2002.

67 M. Taylor, 'Much Shorter Working Weeks Needed to Tackle Climate Crisis – Study', *The Guardian*, 22 May 2019.

68 F. Perera, 'Pollution from Fossil-Fuel Combustion Is the Leading Environmental Threat to Global Pediatric Health and Equity: Solutions Exist', *International Journal of Environmental Research and Public Health*, December 2017.

69 X. Zhang, X. Chen and X. Zhang, 'The Impact of Exposure to Air Pollution on Cognitive Performance', *PNAS*, September 2018.

70 G. Monbiot, 'Toxic Fumes Threaten Our Children: Why Don't We Act?', *The Guardian*, 9 January 2019.

71 D. Carrington, 'Indoor and Outdoor Air Pollution "Claiming at Least 40,000 UK Lives a Year"', *The Guardian*, 22 February 2016.

72 D. Carrington, 'Air Pollution Deaths Are Double Previous Estimates, Finds Research', *The Guardian*, 12 March 2019.

73 'At COP24: Group of 415 Investors Call on World Leaders to Address Climate Change', UNEP Finance Initiative, 10 December 2018.

74 I. Parry, V. Mylonas and N. Vernon, 'Mitigation Policies for the Paris Agreement: An Assessment for G20 Countries', IMF Working Paper, Washington DC, 2018.

75 The Canadian government's scheme has been opposed by Conservative governments in four provinces, siding with the oil industry.

76 A. Fremstad and M. Paul, 'A Short-Run Distributional Analysis of a Carbon Tax in the United States', Political Economy Research Institute Working Paper No. 434, University of Massachusetts, Amherst, August 2017.

77 D. Klenert, L. Mattauch, E. Combet, O. Edenhofer, C. Hepburn, R. Rafaty and N. Stern, 'Making Carbon Pricing Work for Citizens', *Nature Climate Change* 8, 2018, pp. 669–77.

78 J. Hickel, 'Why Growth Can't Be Green', *Foreign Policy*, 12 September 2018.

79 K. Rawlinson, 'British People Do More than £1tn of Housework Each Year – Unpaid', *The Guardian*, 3 October 2018.

80 'Economists' Statement on Carbon Dividends', *Wall Street Journal Opinion*, 20 January 2019.

81 N. Frohlich and J. A. Oppenheimer, *Choosing Justice: An Experimental Approach to Ethical Theory*, Berkeley: University of California Press, 1992.

Chapter 2

1 Eurofound (European Foundation for the Improvement of Living and Working Conditions), *Access to Social Benefits: Reducing Non-Take-Up* (Luxembourg: Publications Office of the European Union, 2015).

2 P. Butler, 'MPs to Launch Inquiry into "Survival Sex" by Benefit Claimants', *The Guardian*, 19 March 2019.

3 Welfare Conditionality Project, *Final Findings Report: Welfare Conditionality Project 2013–2018*, Department of Social Policy and Social Work, University of York, June 2018.

4 National Audit Office, *Benefit Sanctions*, HC 628, Session 2016–17, House of Commons, November 2016.

5 Reported in *The Guardian*, 17 March 2017, p. 16.

6 Department for Work and Pensions, *Guidance: Jobseeker's Allowance Sanctions: How to Keep Your Benefit Payment*, December 2016.

7 D. Webster, 'Benefit Sanctions: Britain's Secret Penal System', Centre for Crime and Justice Studies, 26 January 2015, at https://www.crimeandjusti ce.org.uk/resources/benefit-sanctions-britains-secret-penal-system

8 National Audit Office, *Rolling Out Universal Credit*, HC 1123, Session 2017–19, House of Commons, June 2018.

9 B. Hughes, 'Stormont Buys 40 Cakes to Celebrate Universal Credit', *Irish News*, 10 December 2018.

10 P. Morgan-Bentley, S. Coates and L. Goddard, 'Charities Gagged by Ministers', *The Times*, 12 October 2018, p. 1.

11 The Scottish government has also described sanctions to enforce conditionality as deplorable. Scottish Government, 'Creating a Fairer Scotland: A New Future for Social Security in Scotland', Cabinet Secretary for Social Justice, Communities, and Pensioners' Rights, Edinburgh, 2016.

12 J. Morris, 'Personal Independence Payments: "Statistical Norms" and the Fight to Come', jennymorris.blogspot.com, 2 November 2017.

13 J. Pring, 'The PIP Files: Nearly One in Three Capita Assessments Were Flawed, Reports Reveal', Disability News Service, 8 February 2018.

14 M. Stewart, *Cash not Care: The Planned Demolition of the UK Welfare State*, London: New Generation Publishing, 2016.

15 Press Association, 'DWP Spent £100m on Disability Benefit Appeals, Figures Reveal', *The Guardian*, 12 February 2018, p. 10.

16 'DWP Forced to Admit More Than 111,000 Benefit Deaths', Welfare Weekly, 15 August 2018.

17 For an excellent analysis that addresses the fears of those with disabilities, see J. Elder-Woodward and S. Duffy, *An Emancipatory Welfare State: How Basic Income Might Underpin the Development of Human Potential*, Sheffield: Citizen Network, 2018.

Chapter 3

1 For an elaboration of this function, see Standing, *Basic Income*, pp. 100–2.

2 Thus, American economist Jo Stiglitz, in one of his fleeting visits to the UK, said dismissively, 'Basic income is a cop out. I do not believe it is what people want.' He cited no evidence.

3 Frohlich and Oppenheimer, *Choosing Justice*.

4 A similar approach was taken in a series of national surveys designed by
   this writer and conducted by the International Labour Organization, which
   yielded strong and widespread support for an anchor of basic income. ILO,
   Economic Security for a Better World, Geneva: ILO, 2004.

5 R. Fitzgerald, 'Survey Reveals Young People More Likely to Support Basic
   Income', The Conversation, 17 November 2017.

6 A. Hirschmann, *The Rhetoric of Reaction: Perversity, Futility, Jeopardy*,
   Cambridge, MA: Harvard University Press, 1991.

7 Costing of a basic income system to replace most existing means-tested
   social assistance schemes has been done by the Citizen's Basic Income
   Trust, mainly by its director, Malcolm Torry, drawing on a well-established
   simulation model, Euromod. M. Torry, *The Feasibility of Citizen's Income*,
   London: Palgrave Macmillan, 2016. M. Torry, 'An Update, a Correction,
   and an Extension, of an Evaluation of an Illustrative Citizen's Basic Income
   Scheme', Euromod Working Paper EM12/17a, Institute for Social and
   Economic Research, University of Essex, March 2018.

8 A. Harrop, *For Us All: Redesigning Social Security for the 2020s*, London:
   Fabian Society, 2016.

9 A. Stirling and S. Arnold, *Nothing Personal: Replacing the Personal Tax
   Allowance with a Weekly National Allowance*, London: New Economics
   Foundation, 2019.

10 A. Stirling, 'Universal Basic Income Only Goes so Far – Free Public Services
    Are Essential Too', *The Guardian*, 19 March 2019.

11 K. Buck and D. Gaffney, 'The Practical Response to Our Society's Widening
    Inequality? A Partial Basic Income', Left Foot Forward, 3 September 2018.

12 Harrop, *For Us All*.

13 G. Nixon, 'House Sales, Pensions and the Personal Allowance', ThisIsMoney.
    co.uk, 18 May 2019.

14 M. B. Mansour, 'New Ranking Reveals Corporate Tax Havens Behind
    Breakdown of Global Corporation Tax System; Toll of UK's Tax War
    Exposed', Tax Justice, 28 May 2019.

15 Geoff Crocker has presented a series of papers elaborating on this
    argument. Other commentators have embraced something similar,
    including a group at the New Economics Foundation, Larry Elliott of *The*

Guardian, Martin Wolf of the *Financial Times*, Adair Turner, former chair of the Financial Services Authority, and Anatole Kaletsky, current chair of the Institute for New Economic Thinking.

16 S. Lansley and H. Reed, *A Basic Income for All: From Desirability to Feasibility*, London: Compass, January 2019.

17 For an important contribution to the fund approach, see A. Painter, J. Thorold and J. Cooke, *Pathways to a Universal Basic Income*, London: Royal Society of Arts, 2018.

18 C. Roberts and M. Lawrence, *Our Common Wealth: A Citizens Wealth Fund for the UK*, London: IPPR, 2018.

19 Standing, *Plunder of the Commons*.

20 World Bank, *World Development Report: The Future of Work*, Washington DC: World Bank, October 2018, p. 111.

21 I. Marinescu, 'No Strings Attached: The Behavioral Effects of U.S. Unconditional Cash Transfer Programs', Roosevelt Institute, New York, May 2018.

22 A. Leigh, 'Who Benefits from the Earned Income Tax Credit? Incidence among Recipients, Co-workers and Firms', *The B.E. Journal of Economic Analysis and Policy* 10 (1), May 2010; A. Nichols and J. Rothstein, 'The Earned Income Tax Credit', NBER Working Paper, National Bureau of Economic Research, Washington DC, May 2015.

Chapter 4

1 The idea of 'demonstration projects' is gaining popularity in the United States among Democrats.

2 S. Davala, R. Jhabvala, S. K. Mehta and G. Standing, *Basic Income: A Transformative Policy for India*, London: Bloomsbury, 2015.

3 Note that without changes to taxes, this design would be slightly regressive if applied nationally.

4 A scrupulous estimate for the Citizen's Basic Income Trust showed that a national scheme that provided a basic income of £63 per week to every working-age adult, added £20 to Child Benefit for each child, reduced the income tax personal allowance and the Primary Earnings Threshold for National Insurance contributions to zero and charged National Insurance contributions at 12% across the earnings range, would require an increase in income tax rates of just 3 percentage points. But, of course, there is no need to rely on income tax to pay for that. Torry, 'An Update, a Correction, and an Extension, of an Evaluation of an Illustrative Citizen's Basic Income Scheme'.

5 There are two other options: (1) Different amounts paid in several areas (e.g. £50 in one area, £75 in another) to see if that affects behaviour and attitudes. In principle, this writer is opposed to this. (2) Proceed by inviting locals to participate, and then select from those 'volunteering'. This is also dubious, partly due to selectivity bias.

6 A. B. Atkinson, *Inequality: What Can Be Done?*, London and Cambridge, MA: Harvard University Press, 2015, chapter 8.

7 Torry, *The Feasibility of Citizen's Income*, pp. 134–9.

8 For a fuller critique, see 'Symposium: Anthony Atkinson's "The Case for a Participation Income"', *Political Quarterly* 89(2), April–June 2018; Standing, *Basic Income*, pp. 175–6; M. Torry, *Why We Need a Citizen's Basic Income* (Bristol: Policy Press, 2018), pp. 187–9.

9 D. Willetts, 'Intergenerational Warfare: Who Stole the Millennials' Future?', *Financial Times*, 3 July 2019.

10 R. Partington, 'Most Help-to-Buy Recipients Could Already Afford a Home', *The Guardian*, 13 June 2019.

11 L. Barney, 'Guaranteed Income Preferred Over Lump Sums', Plansponsor. com, 25 October 2018.

12 This section draws on experience in designing and conducting pilots in other countries and on the Appendix to Standing, *Basic Income*, pp. 301–15, as well as on Charlie Young's dissertation and work for the Royal Society of Arts. C. Young, *Making Sense of Basic Income: Clarifying and Classifying the Many Experimental Iterations of a Transformational Policy*, MA Dissertation, Schumacher College, Plymouth University, 2018.

13 J. Doward, A. Walker and M. Savage, 'Revealed: How Universal Credit Is Fuelling Britain's Homelessness Crisis', *The Guardian*, 28 October 2018.

14 Among social scientists, the currently most popular approach is Randomised Control Trial (RCT) methodology that 'treats' a random sample of individuals and compares outcomes with a matched sample

of individuals. A pure RCT along these lines would nevertheless be inappropriate for a basic income pilot. If one individual in a household were provided with a basic income and others were not, there would be a variable degree of sharing and even resentment. If one household received it, and the next-door neighbour did not, similar pressures would arise.

15 The Indian pilots included a post-final evaluation survey, to see what happened once the receipt of basic income stopped, and a legacy survey conducted three years afterwards, primarily to see what recidivism had occurred and what changes were sustained or continued to grow.

16 M. Brown, 'Universal Basic Income: Sheffield Is Largest UK City Yet to Support Trial', *Inverse*, 12 June 2019; H. Gold, 'Sheffield Council Backs Universal Basic Income Trial', *The Guardian*, 12 June 2019.

17 The Scottish part of the Institute for Public Policy Research has attacked the proposal for a basic income in Scotland, claiming it would not reduce child poverty, to which RSA Scotland has responded robustly. A. Learmonth, 'Scots Activists Dismiss Claims UBI Would Cause More Child Poverty', *The National*, 31 May 2018.

18 See, for example, Scottish Basic Income Steering Group, *Exploring the Practicalities of a Basic Income Pilot*, Dunfermline, Fife: Carnegie UK Trust, January 2019.

19 See, for instance, L. Riddoch, 'Scotland Should Ignore Scaremongers and Be Basic Income Pioneers', *The National*, 30 August 2018.

Chapter 5

1 Readers are spoiled for choice of recent books and articles. See, for instance, H. Reed and S. Lansley, *It's Basic Income: The Global Debate*, London: Compass, 2016; Standing, *Basic Income*; Torry, *Why We Need a Citizen's Basic Income*; P. van Parijs and Y. Vanderborght, *Basic Income: A Radical Proposal for a Free Society and a Sane Economy*, Cambridge, MA: Harvard University Press, 2017.

2 P. Collinson, 'Renting? You're Lucky to Have £23 Left After Paying the Bills', *The Guardian*, 9 June 2018.

Appendix A

1 These are covered in more detail in Standing, *Basic Income*, chapter 11.

2 E. Forget, 'The Town With No Poverty: The Health Effects of a Canadian Guaranteed Annual Income Field Experiment', *Canadian Public Policy* 37 (3), 2011, pp. 283–305.

3 D. Calinitsky and J. P. Latner, 'Basic Income in a Small Town: Understanding the Elusive Effects on Work', *Social Problems* 64 (3), 2017, pp. 373–97.

4 Hillary Clinton wrote in her campaign memoir that she had been attracted by the idea of generalizing a commitment to basic income through an 'Alaska for America' plan. She seemed to regret the fact that she lacked the nerve to say so.

5 *The Economist*, 'Free Exchange: We the Shareholders', 22 September 2018, p. 62.

6 Standing, *Plunder of the Commons*, chapter 8.

7 For a review of the numerous schemes, see Standing, *Basic Income*, chapter 10.

8 Among other outcomes, see Davala et al., *Basic Income*.

9 J. Hough and B. Rice, *Providing Personalised Support to Rough Sleepers*, London: Joseph Rowntree Foundation, 2010.

10 KELA, 'From Ideas to Experiment: Report on Universal Basic Income Experiment in Finland', KELA Working Paper 106, Helsinki, 2016.

11 O. Kangas, S. Jauhiainen, M. Simanainen and M. Ylikanno, *The Basic Income Experiment 2017–2018 in Finland: Preliminary Results*, Helsinki: Ministry of Social Affairs and Health, February 2019.

12 M. Ylikanno and O. Kangas, 'Finnish Basic Income Experiment Reveals Problems of Conditional Benefits', *Basic Income News*, 14 April 2019.

13 A. Chakrabortty, 'A Basic Income for Everyone? Yes, Finland Shows It Really Can Work', *The Guardian*, 31 October 2017.

14 *Yie News*, 'Finland's Basic Income Trial: A Springboard for Bolder Experiments?' 5 May 2019.

15 The minister responsible did not say why it was ended. She merely stated that it was 'clearly not the answer for Ontario families', without giving any reasons for that being the case.

16 See, for instance, E. Paling and D. Tencer, 'These Towns Are Trying Out a Basic Income Scheme and It Is Already Changing Lives', *Huffington Post*, 5 June 2018.

17 R. van der Veen, 'Basic Income Experiments in the Netherlands', mimeo., 2018.

18 National League of Cities and Stanford Basic Income Lab, *Basic Income in Cities: A Guide to City Experiments and Pilot Projects*, Stanford, CA, November 2018.

19 T. M. Shapiro and R. Loya, 'Michael Tubbs on Universal Basic Income: "The Issue With Poverty Is a Lack of Cash"', *The Guardian*, 21 March 2019.

20 K. G. Noble, 'What Inequality Does to the Brain', *Scientific American* 316 (3), March 2017, pp. 44–9.

21 C. E. Martin, 'Baby Steps Toward Guaranteed Incomes and Racial Justice', *New York Times*, 8 May 2019.

Appendix B

1 This discussion draws on G. Standing, 'Why a Job Guarantee Is a Bad Joke for the Precariat and for Freedom', Open Democracy, 7 September 2018.

2 'The Guardian View on a Job Guarantee: A Policy Whose Time Has Come', *The Guardian*, 3 May 2018; P. Gregg and R. Layard, 'A Job Guarantee', London School of Economics, 2009.

3 For a critique, see G. Standing, 'Why a Basic Income Is Necessary for a Right to Work', *Basic Income Studies* 7 (2), 2013, pp. 19–40.

4 M. Sandbu, 'Free Lunch Economics: Jobs Guarantee Is a Distant Second-Best Policy', *Financial Times*, 2 July 2018.

5 K. Aronoff, 'Rep. Ro Khanna to Introduce Compromise "Jobs for All" Bill', The Intercept, 30 May 2018.

6 In the United States, the situation is just as bad. It is estimated that about half its 148 million workers earn less than $15 an hour. Imagine if a large proportion of those quit in hope of obtaining a guaranteed better-paying job.

7 E. Loomis, 'The Case for a Federal Jobs Guarantee', *New York Times*, 25 April 2018.

8 L. Summers, 'A Jobs Guarantee – Progressives' Latest Big Idea', *Financial Times*, 2 July 2018.

9 G. Standing, *A Precariat Charter: From Denizens to Citizens*, London and New York: Bloomsbury, 2014.

10 J. Dorfman, 'Job Guarantee: A Liberal Idea That Conservatives May Embrace', *Forbes Magazine*, 1 May 2018.

11 G. Standing, *Work after Globalization: Building Occupational Citizenship*, Cheltenham: Edward Elgar, 2009.

12 S. McElwee, C. McAuliffe and J. Green, 'Why Democrats Should Embrace a Federal Jobs Guarantee', *The Nation*, 20 March 2018.

Appendix C

1 This discussion draws on G. Standing, 'Why "Universal Basic Services" Is No Alternative to Basic Income', Open Democracy, 6 June 2019.

2 A. Coote, P. Kasliwal and A. Percy, *Universal Basic Services: Theory and Practice: A Literature Review*, London: Institute for Global Prosperity, University College London, May 2019.

3 For what seems the most comprehensive advocacy statement of universal basic services, see Social Prosperity Network Report, *Social Prosperity for the Future: A Proposal for Universal Basic Services*, London: University College London, 2017.

4 A penetrating critique concluded that what is being proposed amounts to 'targeted living cost support'. A. Painter, 'Book Review: UCL Institute for Global Prosperity Report Suggesting Universal Basic Services', Citizen's Basic Income Trust, 17 October 2017.

5 UCL Institute for Global Prosperity, 'IGP's Social Prosperity Network Publishes the UK's First Report on Universal Basic Services', Press Release, 11 October 2017, p. 4.

6 The Department for Work and Pensions itself estimates that going from means-tested benefits into the sort of low-paid job claimants could obtain results in only a 20% increase in net income – a poverty trap of 80%. If they also lost 'free food', the net gain would be even less. The precarity trap relates to the long delays between needing benefits and receiving them, a severe disincentive to taking a short-term job that would entail loss of benefits and subsequent risk of being without any income when the job comes to an end.

7 If the one free meal were to be 'dinner', does that mean breakfast and lunch are not considered 'basic'? Let the poor eat once a day, say our new state paternalists.

8 Coote, Kasliwal and Percy, *Universal Basic Services: Theory and Practice.*

9 House of Commons Health and Social Care and Housing, Communities and Local Government Committees, *Long-Term Funding of Adult Social Care*, HC 768, Session 2017–19, House of Commons, June 2018, p. 35.

10 H. Quilter-Pinner and D. Hochlaf, *Social Care: Free at the Point of Need* (London: Institute for Public Policy Research, May 2019).

11 L. Buckner and S. Yeandle, *Valuing Carers 2015: The Rising Value of Carers' Support*, London: Carers UK, 2015, also cited in House of Commons Health and Social Care and Housing, Communities and Local Government Committees, *Long-Term Funding of Adult Social Care*, p. 11.

12 House of Commons Health and Social Care and Housing, Communities and Local Government Committees, *Long-Term Funding of Adult Social Care*, p. 40.

13 Evidence for this was revealed in basic income pilots in India and in recent assessments in the UK. See, for instance, Davala et al., *Basic Income*; G. Standing, *Basic Income as Common Dividends: Piloting a Transformative Policy. A Report for the Shadow Chancellor of the Exchequer*, London: Progressive Economy Forum, May 2019.

14 A. Percy, 'Forget the Universal Basic Income – Here's an Idea That Would Truly Transform Our Society', *Left Foot Forward*, 15 October 2018.

15 See, for instance, Percy, 'Forget the Universal Basic Income'.

16 Cited in A. Grant, 'Universal Basic Income Is Attempt to "Euthanise the Working Class as a Concept"', *The Herald* (Scotland), 17 August 2018.

17 For a review of evidence gathered in over 30 years of research and the conduct of pilots in many places, see Standing, *Basic Income.*

18 A. Coote with E. Yazici, *Universal Basic Income: A Union Perspective* (New Economics Foundation and Public Services International,

April 2019), p. 37. This so-called study could not cite a single British trade unionist in support of its hostility to basic income, and the only British union mentioned has actually come out in favour. Calling the report a 'union perspective' is analogous to calling the services proposal 'universal'.

19 In drawing up a Precariat Charter of desirable policies, I proposed that everybody should have the right to financial advice, vital in a complex financialized system. Standing, *A Precariat Charter*.

Index